THE NATION IN THE SCHOOLS

Wanted: A Canadian Education

Rowland M. Lorimer

Research in Education Series / 11

OISE Press / The Ontario Institute for Studies in Education
Canadian Learning Materials Centre/Centre de ressources
pédagogiques canadiennes

The Ontario Institute for Studies in Education has three prime functions: to conduct programs of graduate study in education, to undertake research in education, and to assist in the implementation of the findings of educational studies. The Institute is a college chartered by an Act of the Ontario Legislature in 1965. It is affiliated with the University of Toronto for graduate studies purposes.

The publications program of the Institute has been established to make available information and materials arising from studies in education, to foster the spirit of critical inquiry, and to provide a forum for the exchange of ideas about education. The opinions expressed should be viewed as those of the contributors.

©The Ontario Institute for Studies in Education 1984
252 Bloor Street West
Toronto, Ontario M5S 1V6

Canadian Cataloguing in Publication Data

Lorimer, Rowland, 1944-
The nation in the schools : wanted: a Canadian education

(Research in education series ; 11)
Co-published by Ontario Institute for Studies in
Education and Canadian Learning Materials Centre
ISBN 0-7744-0271-7

1. Education, Elementary — Canada — Curricula.
2. Canada — Civilization — Study and teaching
(Elementary). I. Ontario Institute for Studies in
Education. II. Canadian Learning Materials Centre. III. Title. IV. Series

LB1564.C3L67 1984   372.19′0971   C84-098768-4

ISBN 0-7744-0271-7   Printed in Canada
1 2 3 4 5 WC 88 78 68 58 48

Contents

Foreword

This book is the result of a close collaboration between Professor Rowland Lorimer and the Canadian Learning Materials Centre. Since the subject of Dr. Lorimer's research closely matched the objectives of the Centre, and since the Centre contained the only comprehensive collection of Canadian learning materials (over 7000 titles) in the country, it seemed appropriate that we should work closely together. Dr. Lorimer was invited, therefore, to spend his half-year sabbatical from Simon Fraser University as a Research Fellow of the Centre, where he completed the manuscript for *The Nation in the Schools*.

The Canadian Learning Materials Centre is a national, independent organization whose mandate is to promote a Canadian context for public school education. Its basic aim has been to try to relate what one might term the politics of education to the politics of publishing. By devising policies and programs that will improve the quality and variety of regional and national learning materials, the Centre attempts to contribute towards a strong and independent publishing industry in Canada.

Specifically, *The Nation in the Schools* provides a survey of Canadian content in language arts, literature, and social studies curricula. It analyses the procedures used in the selection of learning materials and teacher training programs and addresses the degree to which they foster the dissemination of Canadian content in the classroom. Finally, Professor Lorimer suggests strategies to encourage and ensure a thoroughly Canadian context to the formal curriculum of our nations' schools.

This book has been co-published by the CLMC and OISE Press with the assistance of the Canada Council, because we feel it contributes to the general understanding of the issues involved in the development of Canadian learning materials. We believe it provides a valuable complement to Paul Robinson's *Publishing for Canadian Classrooms*, a CLMC publication now being used in teacher education courses across the country. *The*

Nation in the Schools also provides important information on changes which are currently being introduced in the curriculum. Finally, it offers a broad discussion and policy analysis of decisions which determine publisher participation, Canadian content, and the cultural orientation of Canadian education. Most of all, however, it is a nagging reminder that our nation's survival lies in the classrooms of this country.

Michael MacDonald, Chairman, CLMC Board
Ann Brimer, Director, CLMC

Preface

The issues raised in this book can be seen in a narrow framework. They can be said to be the consequences of the particular history of Canadian culture and institutions, constitutional arrangements, and the proclivities of a particular profession. Perceived in such a manner, they can be viewed as solvable through awareness, policy initiatives, institutional changes, and determination.

However, my view is, and it has strengthened as I have researched and written this book, that the patterns of the creation, production, and dissemination of educational information, discussed herein, are manifestations of a firmly entrenched, broadly based information order. The identified patterns and implications are readily translatable into any area of culture or communication, any socially oriented profession, and any set of institutions.

A UNESCO commission report, entitled *Many Voices One World*, which has come to be known as the MacBride Report, has discussed these problems in a broad context. It calls for the redressing of inequities in information generation and information flows under a rubric referred to as a "new world information order." Intrinsic to such a new order would be mechanisms which would allow nations to use communications for their development needs. It would prevent other more powerful nations from imposing their plan for development upon the consciousness of a people and hence the fabric of a nation other than their own.

The principles which are current in the global exchange of information, whether in education or journalism, are so at variance with this plea for fundamental respect for pluralism and particular cultures that the MacBride Report has caused a major rift in UNESCO. The United States has presently withdrawn its considerable funding from the organization, while the nations of the Third World plow ahead with implementation plans which are fraught with problems for the freedom of individual human beings, the development of tolerant communities, and for civilization writ large.

There is no reason to assume that the path towards a culturally based education in Canada will be any the less difficult than the addressing of global information inequities. Nor is the achievement of such an education any less important than that global struggle. As Senator Michael Pitfield and the former Chair of the Economic Council of Canada, Sylvia Ostry, argue about how to integrate the Canadian and American economies, the cultural sector becomes increasingly important if only because it may be all that we will have left. Even there some doubt arises. Ms. Ostry would give the information sector over to free trade, a move which could severely hamper every intiative conceived of in this book.

Within education, as ever, culturally sensitive moves are continually initiated even while others neutralize them. As the Maritime premiers seek approval for acts in their respective legislatures designed to encourage the development of regionally sensitive learning materials, some multinationals busy themselves in making agreements with local publishers to make joint submissions for the contract to develop those materials. While year by year small increments occur in the number of Canadian-written and -published books on social science and humanities university courses and in university bookstores, the University of Ottawa joins in a partnership with an American college bookstore chain forbidden by the Federal Investment Review Agency to operate the university bookstore under lease. The purpose of the partnership, when all is said and done, is to use the American market expertise of the chain to stock a selection of book and non-book merchandise that will allow the store to operate in the black. So much for Canadian books.

Similar countercurrents are running elsewhere. As some provincial governments see the opportunity of encouraging Canadian technology through adopting Canadian microcomputers, Apple Canada Inc. begins to align Canadian educational researchers with grants for the development of materials and the study of materials compatible with the Apple computer. And as universities struggle for budgets to carry forward programs sometimes at double and triple the class load of five years ago, American university consortia begin to beam video-based university courses up to satellites which, if not aimed at Canada, certainly spill over into the geographical areas in which most of us live.

A Canadian imagination and a Canadian knowledge base in the population as a whole will not survive untended. Their nurturing will require a determination to challenge curriculum construction and implementation, classroom practice, subject definition and orientation, professional attitudes, activities and training, the procedures of creation and selection of learning materials, the right of participation in the educational market place, and even the basic principles of twentieth-century pedagogy.

Nor will this challenge be easy. Even if Ms. Ostry fails to give away the whole game just as we begin, our policies and determination will be tested from within and without by the ideas and interests of those who trade in the present order. Rights to do business and the wisdom of professions are sacred cows to take on in the name of any cause. And cultural survival in Canada is not the strongest of rallying cries.

Interestingly and somewhat paradoxically our inherited cultural weakness in education may prove to be a future strength. Whatever the federal government decides on free trade, it cannot give away what falls within the jurisdiction of the provinces. While some provinces cannot rely upon provincial administrators to take up a cultural perspective, some, notably Quebec, Ontario, and probably the Atlantic provinces, can. But perhaps more telling in the cultural scene will be new developments. As social science and education academics get called into the service of various levels of government for their research capabilities, their awareness of the cultural dimension may increase. To put it another way, as the intellectual, governing, and business elites are necessarily drawn closer together by an increasingly complex, information-hungry society, alliances and allegiances may provide cultural nationalists with a competitive edge.

Acknowledgments

This work has been long in its evolution. In the initial research I was invaluably aided by Margaret Long. James Lorimer helped me develop those investigations into a larger work. Various individuals were encouraging of the research, including Paul Heyer, Philip Jones, Alan and Carmen Luke, Michael Manley-Casimir, Jack Quarter, Paul Robinson, Ed Sullivan, and Tony Wilden. I am extremely grateful to the Canadian Learning Materials Centre at Dalhousie University for providing me with various types of support in working towards a final draft, not the least of which was a unique and invaluable library. John Henninger-Shuh, Peter Kidd, Michael MacDonald, and Douglas Myers helped transform my stay at the Centre into one that was personally enriching. Oddly enough, for the first time in my professional career, I was afforded the wonderful opportunity to work with colleagues who shared the same commitment and priorities on the same subject matter.

I have also had the benefit of comments from a variety of people in academics, education, and publishing. Particular thanks are due again to most of those mentioned above and Pat Barnes, Arden Ford, Norman Horrocks, John Irwin, Basil McDermott, Gladys Neale, Libby Oughton, Glenda Redden, Bob Reid, George Tomkins, Lisa Underwood, and Tom Wilkinson. Of course, any weaknesses, errors, or misinterpretations are my own responsibility.

The bulk of the research for this book was conducted without the aid of any formal research grant. However, towards the end of the research three agencies provided considerable assistance. The SSHRC provided a sabbatical grant, the Canadian Learning Materials Centre provided a base of operations, and the Canada Council assisted with the publication and distribution of this book.

A special acknowledgment needs to go to typist extraordinaire Lucie Menkveld for her continual willingness to type yet another version of a chapter both quickly and accurately.

I have spent almost my entire life in close proximity to educators involved in schooling. But I have always kept my distance. They and their institutions I find intriguing, and while I have any disagreements with their priorities they have my respect. Most significantly, I am continually impressed by their humanity.

I would like to dedicate this book to my family, Anne Carscallen, Stefan Carscallen, Conor Rowland James, and to those, if any, yet to appear corporeally.

Rowland Moore Lorimer
Coquitlam, British Columbia

Introduction

1839   Until Canada is nationalized and Anglified it is idle for England to be devising schemes for her improvement. In this great work of nationalization, education is at once the most convenient and powerful instrument.

— Lord Durham, from G. Craig, *Lord Durham's Report* (Ottawa: Carleton Library Series, 1963), p. 150.

1840s   In precisely those parts of Upper Canada where the American school books had been used most extensively, there the spirit of the insurrection in 1837 and 1838 was the most prevalent.

— Egerton Ryerson, from J. D. Wilson, "Education in Upper Canada: Sixty Years of Change," in J.D. Wilson, R. Stamp, and L. Audet (eds.) *Canadian Education: A History* (Toronto: Prentice Hall, 1970), p. 209.

1867   It is quite clear to me that if we are to succeed with our new Dominion, it can never be by accepting a ready-made easy literature, which assumes Bostonian culture to be the worship of the future, and the American democratic system to be the manifestly destined form of government for all the civilized world, new as well as old.

— Thomas D'Arcy McGee, "The Mental Outfit of the New Dominion" (1867), in C. Ballstadt, *The Search for English-Canadian Literature* (Toronto: University of Toronto Press, 1975), pp. 94-95.

1951   The uncritical use of American training institutions and therefore of American educational philosophy and . . . teaching aids has certainly tended to make our education system less Canadian, less suited to our traditions.

. . . How many Canadians realize that over a large part of Canada the schools are accepting tacit direction from New York (Columbia University) that they would not think of taking from Ottawa?

— The Massey Commission, in V. Massey, *Royal Commission on Arts, Letters and Sciences* (Ottawa: King's Printer, 1951), pp. 15-16.

1968   Let us frankly recognise that what we are teaching our young people about Canada and its problems is antiquated. The courses of study in Canadian history are based on the interests and concerns that preoccupied academic historians of the 1920s. These courses lack contemporary meaning.

— A. B. Hodgetts, *What Culture? What Heritage?* (Toronto: OISE, 1968), p. 115.

1972   It is enough to say here that while our educational system has been developing its present admirable flexibility, the *de facto* displacement of Canadian textbooks in our schools by foreign learning materials of every kind has been proceeding apace.

— Ontario Royal Commission on Book Publishing, in R. Rohmer, D. Camp, and M. Jeanneret, *Canadian Publishers and Canadian Publishing* (Toronto: Royal Commission on Book Publishing, Queen's Printer, 1972), p.76.

1975   In distinction from most other comparable industrialized countries, Canada has neither produced a politically motivated educational reform, rooted in a conception of the country's future nor has Canada blocked such reform. . . . Canada has exceptionally active programs . . . that are . . . derived from no explicitly stated, overall national conception of the country's interests.

— Organization for Economic Co-operation and Development. *External Examiners Report on Educational Policy in Canada* (Toronto: Canadian Association for Adult Education), 1975.

1979   The provinces should emphasize that education has a Canada-wide dimension by giving prominence to Canadian studies, and they should through a strengthened Council of Ministers of Education, develop ways and means by which this dimension may be represented in our school systems.

— The Report of the Task Force on Canadian Unity, in J. L. Pepin and J. Roberts, *A Future Together* (Ottawa: Task Force on Canadian Unity, Ministry of Supply and Services), 1979.

Education has not been conducted from within a national cultural framework in Canada. Indeed, the cultural and political nature of Canadian education, that aspect which ties education to what is distinctive about the community of which it is a part, has been sorely neglected.

This neglect has often been attributed to the division of powers by the British North America Act, now the Canada Act. In giving the major responsibilities for education to the provinces, Canada's constitution has emphasized the administration rather than the conceptualization of education. Obviously, education need not be conceived ten times over within one country. However, decisions on curriculum, decisions on professional training, and decisions on the adoptions of learning materials are made ten times over. And since policies require rationales, we get very close to conceiving of education education ten times over. While the provinces cling to their right to control their fragment of the national market, educational publishers create materials increasingly aimed at an international market. The result is that as the publishing industry expands its geographical boundaries, the preset geographical boundaries and therefore the market size the provinces possess as a bargaining tool to command distinctive materials weakens. Educational publishers are also developing formats which, if only because of cost, can at best be adapted for countries, not provinces. The result is that geographical constraints of provincial boundaries are increasingly weakening the ability of provinces to withstand international economic forces.

The creation of a co-ordinating body, the Council of Ministers of Education of Canada (CMEC), seems to have been a tentative recognition of the need for interprovincial co-operation, perhaps even a recognition of the shifting balance of power in the making of educational decisions out of the hands of educators and into the hands of publishers. However, the CMEC has not encouraged a multitude of co-operative projects working towards an appropriate level of regional and national integration and hence increased market power. The CMEC seems to have been limited by its member provinces to providing information between provinces so that accidental parallels do not go unrecognized. The relinquishing of provincial autonomy for the sake of broader cultural/educational goals has been halting indeed.

But as halting as progress towards co-ordinated action in education has been, too much can be made of the constitutional issue. Other countries such as Britain, New Zealand, and Australia do not have curricula and learning materials which differ substantially from Canada's in their recognition of national culture. Also, in other Canadian cultural industries, such as broadcasting, which are unencumbered by provincial jurisdiction, the internationalization of professions and cultural products parallels education.

While the constitution may retard the process of moving towards a culturally sensitive education, it need not discourage us from conceiving of education from within a national cultural framework. Nor should it hinder us in identifying other major contributing factors to the cultural denuding of education which are more amenable to change.

The present study examines contemporary Canadian schooling from within a national cultural framework and within the formal political structure which presently exists. Initially, it examines the degree to which national cultural realities exist in provincial curricula. It then turns to the major formative influences on schooling — the professional training of educators and the educational publishing industry — to explain the tenaciousness with which a non-cultural approach grips current educational practices and perspectives. It ends, building upon a growing body of initiatives, with suggestions for reform.

Chapter 1 describes the present state of the language arts and English provincial curricula and the inclusion of Canadian content and Canadian writing. Chapter 2 takes on approximately the same task for social studies. In Chapter 3 teacher training across the nation is examined with respect to its orientation to Canada and Canadian realities. Chapter 4 discusses both the business of educational publishing and the procedures educators use in selecting learning materials for the classroom. Chapter 5 completes the study with recommendations designed to build into Canadian education a permanent Canadian character.

1: Canadian Content in Language Arts

The mind supplies the ideas of a nation but what gives
this idea its sentimental force is a community of dreams.
— André Malraux

The "community of dreams" children encounter in the Canadian school
has more to do with an American belief in individual heroism or British
notions of social order than with any identifiable Canadian dream. There
is very little, in fact, that is Canadian about the reading materials
Canadian educators choose to use in Canadian classrooms.

Canada barely exists as a place in language arts texts used in grades
1 to 3. In grades 4 to 6 it can claim only a tentative place in the curriculum.
While our country does emerge as a concrete geographical and social entity in junior high school, it does so only occasionally, and most often in a
context that tends to trivialize its significance. Even in high school, where
20 percent of the reading material available is Canadian — still a scan-
dalously small percentage — most teachers fail to present the material in
its cultural context.

A number of factors have helped created this distressing situation. At
the elementary level, for example, educators tend to worry far more about
the acquisition of reading and language skills than about the content and
context of the material presented. As a result, they have left such considerations to textbook publishers. The publishers, wanting to gain as large a
share of the market as possible, create books that play down local, regional,
and national cultural content while emphasizing apparently common
values. Too often, this combination produces bland books which concentrate upon upwardly mobile, middle-class North Americans who most often
live in suburban neighborhoods and participate in predictable adventures.

In secondary school, the material itself is generally of a much higher

1

literary quality, but the cultural biases are still those of other places, most notably the United States and Britain. American and British literature is presented simply as "literature" without any indication that it develops from a particular national culture and a particular set of values. Even when Canadian literature is offered, it is presented in the same manner, encouraging not only the illusion that literature is created in a cultural vacuum but also the sense that the ideas and themes of American and British writers are our own themes and ideas.

To understand the details of the current situation, I shall first examine the level of Canadian content in the language arts program of primary grades and the typical and frequently used materials now being taught in English programs in Canadian secondary schools.

Canadian Content in the Primary Grades

In 1981 there were more than fifteen different reading series used in grades 1 to 3 in Canada. In Holt, Rinehart and Winston's *Language Patterns*,[1] a provincially recommended series in British Columbia which is also used in Ontario and other provinces, there were less than 20 specific references to Canada in approximately 130 stories and poems. In Nelson's *Language Development Reading Program*,[2] perhaps the most widely used series across Canada, there were only 17 definite and implied Canadian references in all the grades 1 to 3 material.[3] In typical books from Ginn's *Starting Points in Reading*[4] series, also popular in Ontario, there were no references in 13 stories in one book and one reference in 11 stories in another.

What the editors put in place of Canadian content is a generalized North American world bled of all its significant particulars. Everyone lives in more or less the same way, whether they live in Canada or the United States, on the prairies or by the ocean. Major geographical features of Canada like the Canadian Rockies, the Prairies, Hudson Bay, the St. Lawrence River, and the continental shelf are conspicuous by their almost total absence.

Even street names are not ones peculiar to any set of cities or single city, but are common to nearly every North American city or town. Names and patterns of names with obvious Canadian significance, such as Wolfe, Montcalm, King, Queen, Cartier, MacDonald, Laurier, or even Manitoba or St. Lawrence, are replaced by common names such as Main Street, River Road, or Birch Crescent. Distinctive names such as Bloor, Chebucto, Côte des Neiges, Jasper Avenue, Portage, Granville, or even Jinglepot Road are absent.

Against this non-specific backdrop of a generalized neighborhood with no ethnic or geographical particularities, children learn about the activities and amusements of a mythical set of middle class or upwardly striving, nuclear families who come from no discernible roots or culture.

The prose material, which provides the backbone of the content of the readers, is centred around a few characters that change from story to story, but usually include some children, their parents, some friends, neighbors, grandparents, and, like paid mourners, several paid community functionaries.

Government employees are present but rarely in identifiable forms, such as Canada Post or British Columbia Department of Highways. Even Canada's famous police force is rarely portrayed as the RCMP or the Mounties, but just as "the police." Mayors serve as a catch-all category representing the political spectrum to the exclusion of somewhat more distinctive Canadian political positions such as prime minister or provincial premier.

The themes and ideas of the stories complement their settings. They emphasize the adventures and recreational possibilities of everyday, middle-class living. But these excursions do not lead to in-depth studies of any Canadian geographical or cultural element; they are simply small dramas sufficient to underline a specific moral lesson. For example, an abandoned mine may cave in when the children undertake a forbidden visit. The history, geography, geology, and economics of the area, possible focal areas for discussion, are all ignored in favor of following the dramatic force of the story, emphasizing the need for obedience.

Superimposed upon this world that, among others, *Language Patterns* and Copp Clark's *Canadian Reading Development Series* present is a one-dimensional portrayal of interpersonal interaction. Each character is related to every other within a strict status hierarchy. For example, older boys are always portrayed as more competent than younger boys, men over women, boys over girls, and so forth. The stories depict a status hierarchy favoring males and older people (to middle age) that preordain the characteristics and competencies of the people involved. Dad shows everyone how to do it. Big brother has the idea that captivates all the children.

In sum, the primary school book world is non-specific, homogeneous, and simplistic. It might be termed a "generic" world for its basic recognizability but its lack of distinguishing characteristics. It constrains the view children get of themselves, their communities, and their country unnecessarily. What is missing most obviously are the patterns of individuality and variety which children see all around them in the real world, the patterns of individuality and variety which make up the culture of Canada.

Canadian Content at the Intermediate Level

In general, the content of the stories in intermediate readers builds upon primary readers. The settings expand from the immediate vicinity of the family home and family outings to include activities a child of 8 to 11 years might engage in outside the family, such as going to camp, going shopping, or playing community sports. Big brothers no longer outshine their younger siblings on every count, but are presented as different in talent. There are also developments in form. Non-fiction is mixed with fiction, plays, and a wide selection of different kinds of poetry. But, as with the primary readers, the world is extremely restricted. The selections centre around middle-class recreational activities that make sense within the generalized world of the books. For example, something as basic as the realities of the adult working world and its influence on the lives of children are missing totally. So, too often, is Canada.

Several studies have examined the Canadian content of intermediate readers in some cases along with their primary counterparts. A presentation of the data in tables on the following pages helps to point out major patterns in story content which can serve as a touchstone for the discussion to follow.

Table 1.1 shows there to be a major difference in Canadian content both in fiction and non-fiction between some Nelson published books and those published by Ginn.[5] In fiction what is lacking in Canadian content in the Ginn books is not replaced by U.S. content, but by generic, North American content. In non-fiction in one series (*Starting Points*), the replacement pattern is the same for the non-fiction. In *Reading 360*, a series originally developed in the United States, Canadian content is replaced with American content.

Table 1.2, taken from a different study, broadens the number of textbook series examined but confines the analysis to grade 4 readers.[6] It shows the same contrast between the Nelson and Ginn books but also points to a cluster of books of other publishers, four out of five of which contain more American than Canadian content.

Table 1.1 / Geographic Settings of the Fiction of Four Reading Series (percentage)

	Canada	Likely Canada	Any-where N.Amer.	U.S.	Likely U.S.	Cdns Abroad	Others Countries
Nelson (Gr 4-6) *Total (108)	48	38	2	3	0	3	3
Ginn (406) Starting Points (111)	4	4	46	6	3	0	31
Ginn 360 (1-6) Cdn. edn. (155)	5	1	55	9	2	0	28
Ginn 360 (1-6) U.S. edn. (154)	1	0	54	14	2	0	29

Geographic Settings Non-Fiction (percentage)

	Canada	U.S.	N.Amer.	Cdns Abroad	Other Countries	World	World & U.S.
Nelson (4-6) *Total (7)	100	0	0	0	0	0	0
Ginn (4-6) Starting Points (66)	27	7	18	2	27	14	5
Ginn 360 (106) Cdn. edn. (44)	27	47	24	0	5	0	0
Ginn 360 (1-6) U.S. edn. (41)	0	64	29	0	7	0	0

*Total = Total "units", i.e., stories or pieces of non-fiction.

Table1.2/Canadian Content in Canadian Readers, Grade 4 Reading Series (percentage)

Series Publisher and Titles	Canadian Content	American Content	Other Countries	Other
Nelson (Rowboats and Roller-skates; Driftwood and Dandelions; Hockey Cards and Hopscotch)	81	7	3	9
Holt, Rinehart & Winston (Ready or Not . . .)	41	26	17	16
Gage Educational (People Like Me)	24	36	36	4
Ginn (Starting Points in Reading A, First Book and Second Book)	15	42	27	16
Copp Clark (Voyager I)	8	44	29	19
Longman (Brown is the Back of a Toad)	11	43	31	15

Source: Analysis by George Martell and Brina Rose based on the number of items (stories, poems, etc.) in each reading series. Analysis based on the number of pages of text and illustrations does not produce markedly different results.

Figure 1.1 Canadian Authorship of Some Major Reading Programs Listed in Circular 14 (Taken from Toronto Board of Education Study)

	Programs	% of Pages by Canadians
1.	Copp Clark Voyager Program (grades 4-6)	19
	Dent Developing Comprehension in Reading	
2.	(grades 2-3)	95
3.	(grades 4-6)	43
4.	Gage Expressways	80
5.	Gage Strategies for Language Arts (grades 4-6)	37
6.	Ginn Starting Points in Language Arts (grades K-3)	73
7.	Ginn Starting Points in Reading (grades 4-6)	14
8.	Holt Language Patterns Program (K-3)	55
9.	"Hickory Hollow ABC" to "Heads & Tails"	100
10.	"Make-Believe Time" to "Treasure Chest"	89
11.	Nelson Language Developmental Reading Program (4-6)	84
12.	Science Research Associates Individualized Reading Skills Program	71

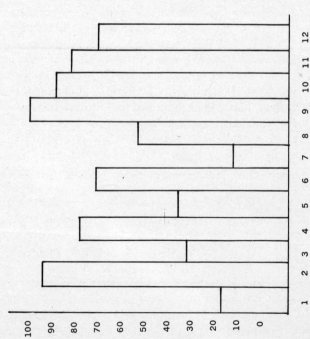

Figure 1.1, taken from a third study, broadens the number of textbook series even further (including some K-3 material) and examines Canadian authorship.[7] A wide range in the percentage of pages written by Canadians is shown roughly correlating with the amount of Canadian content at the 4 to 6 level. The correlation between authorship and content does not hold true for the primary material.

An In-Depth Look at Two Reading Series

The following analysis focusses on the two most widely used series across Canada, Ginn's *Starting Points* and Nelson's *Language Development Reading Program*.

Starting Points

Table 1.1 indicates that in *Starting Points* (grades 4 to 6), 8 percent of the fiction and 27 percent of the non-fiction have Canadian settings. In Table 1.2 we find that 15 percent of the grade 4 material has Canadian content.

A thematic analysis of the prose material of the series explains the context within which this very low level of Canadian content occurs.[8] The world of *Starting Points* is filled with clumsy institutions in an uncaring society that proceeds according to a momentum of its own. This society is arbitrary at best, but often wrong-headed, uncomprehending, unappreciative, and one must struggle against it to survive. Individuals acting alone make situations tolerable by imposing their individual wills on events to produce peace, harmony, growth, and so on.

In the world of *Starting Points*, a homogeneous boundless conglomeration of individuals strive to make their ways, but there is nevertheless a social order. It is conveyed by an implicit single set of rules for behavior, valid for all situations. The key rule is that the arbitrary social momentum of the world demands individual initiative and persistence — *individual* initiative because social groups are portrayed as cumbersome and conflict-ridden, and *persistence* because a character needs considerable will to affect the on-going momentum of society.

The demands of such a role are heavy. In one story at the grade 5 level, for example, a boy has become known as "the bully of Barkham Street." He is portrayed as being a behavior problem partially because both his parents work. There are no descriptions of helpful social groups such as neighborhood parents, the school, the community centre, or peer groups, merely a boy left alone to cope with his own individual misfortune in his own individual way.[9]

In such a simplistic, adversarial world, the very idea of using real institutions is dangerous because it would mean fingering the culprit institutions responsible for foiling the will of individuals. Since *Starting Points* does not want to do that, for libel reasons if none other, institutions are generic rather than specific, for example, the police vs. the RCMP, Phil's Pharmacy vs Shopper's Drug Mart, and so on. So, too, are places. If an antagonistic story happened in a specific place, that might taint the location. While bland stories can be described in specifics (even Canadian specifics), dramatic stories must take place in some non-existent, non-threatening locale.

The end result of the style of presentation *Starting Points* uses is a world without significant concrete realities. It is a world in which specifically Canadian cultural content has no place.

The Language Development Reading Program

In stark contrast to *Starting Points*, as Table 1.1 shows, in Nelson's *Language Development Reading Program* (grades 4 to 6), 86 percent of the fiction and 100 percent of the non-fiction selections have Canadian settings. In Table 1.2 we find that 81 percent of the grade 4 material has Canadian content. It is also — and not incidentally — very different from *Starting Points* in its perspective on the world.

A thematic analysis of the Nelson stories shows that the community is the central focus of the material. A complex statement emerges about the interaction of individuals with the social process, a social process which always has particular attributes. And in this series, those attributes are specifically Canadian.

In the Nelson world the individual is both a person and a member of the social whole. His or her life has its own integrity, but it is enhanced because it contributes to something beyond itself, to social and cultural dimensions of human existence. The individual acts with social consequence. Action is thus placed within a context, and that context is then placed within a broader context. For instance, the local community is placed within the regional or national community. This "nesting" is not merely a pleasant background; it comes to play an active part in forming the outlook both of the individuals within the story and the students who read the materials.

The writers have accomplished this considerable literary feat by outlining in some detail both the singular character of individuals and the specific and concrete attributes of the community. For example, four English Canadian girls invade a French Canadian boy's lakeside paradise. The boy is protective of his turf, the girls are cliquish. The story's setting transforms this rather ordinary situation in which boys and girls do not quite know how to make contact with each other into a story of interpersonal and cultural import. The latter is achieved through the use of the context of French-English tensions.

The Nelson program also shows social change as the consequence of the intentions and actions of individuals acting together. In the story cited above much of the tension between characters arises from their lack of contact. Hostility develops, endangering the life of the boy. But with the

8

intervention of the father of one of the girls, they make contact and a major shift in the relationship between the girls and the boy occurs. Through this story and its resolution, the reader comes to understand some of the dynamics operating (in a microcosm) in Canada's French–English tensions and its potential for change.

Certain advantages follow from specifying the social identity of the characters. The various individuals clearly belong to a given community with its inherited boundaries. This allows for a discussion of the limitations of one set of values or one culture on the one side and, on the other side, of pluralism and multiculturalism. In the example cited, the limitations of French and English Canadian cultures are not presented in the abstract; rather the limitations of the concrete world are defined by the behavior of the boy and the girls. The fun that the two have together when the ice is broken is also made comprehensible.

The Canadian references are not tangential to the action of the stories. Rather they form a bridge to help children relate the dynamics of the story to their own lives. Concrete references to place, people, and institutions become connected to the power of the story just as historical sites become connected to the power of the historical event. At the most general level, they provide a sense of the importance of being in a particular place and a member of a particular community. More concretely they provide a knowledge base for a pride in Canada.

Of course, there is one other strength in including all this concrete Canadian material. With people who have Canadian sensibilities writing about Canadian settings, there is likely to be a close connection between the themes of the reading series and the themes treated in Canadian literature. In the case of the Nelson series, the connection is clear. A person reading Atwood's *Survival: A Thematic Guide to Canadian Literature*,[10] Frye's *The Bush Garden: Essays on the Canadian Imagination*,[11] or Mandel's *Context of Canadian Criticism*[12] would recognize many of the themes within the stories of the Nelson readers as similar to what these critics see as predominant in Canadian literature. The readers, therefore, provide an introduction to the Canadian imagination.

The Special Case of a "Canadianized" Reading Series

Outside Ontario considerable use is made of reading series which are adaptations or "Canadianizations" of series developed in and for foreign countries. One such series, well used in several provinces, is Ginn's *Reading 360*. As Table 1.1 points out, the Canadian content to be found — 6 percent of fiction and 27 percent of non-fiction (contrasted to American content of 9 percent of fiction and 24 percent of non-fiction) — is minimal. Examination of the Canadian and American editions, both the student texts and teacher guides, reveals a great deal about the Canadianization process.

It transpires that the process of Canadianization involves editors and consultants expunging some American references and replacing them with Canadian or neutral references. Occasionally, Canadian material is inserted, but this is rare since it is a very costly process. Very occasionally selections are rewritten usually to cope with problems of space. The result is that the literary quality of the Canadian edition deteriorates because of the deletion of specific references, adaptation and/or condensation of the original work.

In one section of the Canadian edition of *The Sun That Warms*, a section that makes a special point of introducing the authors, most of whom are American, James Daugherty is introduced as follows: "Perhaps Mr. Daugherty's idea of rewriting the old fable in this fashion was inspired by the stories. . . ."[13] In the American edition, the passage reads: "Perhaps as Mr. Daugherty walked between the stone lions at the entrance to the New York Public Library he was reminded of one of the stories . . . ."[14] In a different section of the Canadian edition, a story about a dog was adapted from three stories about three different breeds of dogs. In the American edition, attention is drawn to the specific genetic characteristics of a Bloodhound, a German Shepherd, and a Doberman. In the Canadian edition, those same characteristics become the traits of one German Shepherd. In a selection called "Night Workers" in another book of the series, entitled *All Sorts of Things*, American pupils find accurate figures while Canadians get only vague guesses. "2,500 men and women postal workers" is changed to "hundreds of men and women." They sort "five million letters" in the United States and "thousands of letters and packages" in Canada.[15] In the United States, sixty milk trucks deliver fifty thousand quarts of milk. Those same sixty trucks deliver only two thousand quarts of milk in Canada!

In spite of the changes, a significant American presence remains. We are told, for example: "This is the story of Harriet Tubman, born a slave in Maryland in 1822 who made a daring escape north to freedom. At the risk of her life she returned nineteen times to lead more than 300 of her people to the 'Promised Land'."[16] There is no reference to th considerable Canadian involvement in harboring slaves in either the text or the teacher's guide.

Other examples are just as disturbing. A science selection called "The Dawn Redwood Trees" presents American knowledge and expertise as necessary to the entire world. A Chinese "forester" of pre-revolutionary China brings some unusual needles to an unidentified Chinese institution for identification. The book offers no reason for his particular curiosity, but lack of knowledge of their significance is implied by the absence of an explanation. An American scientist is called in, implicitly indicating that the Chinese need an American to "prove" the identity of the needles. Consequently, our hero, the American scientist-cum-explorer, sets off in company with a San Francisco reporter to get to the trees. Their "harrowing journey" (more harrowing for the porters, who are referred to as "coolies" and who carry the Americans) almost kills the scientist on the way to the "inaccessible and remote" area (not far from a number of Chinese villages).

This story is particularly bad for its implicit racism. But no suggestion is made, even in the teacher's guide, that children should be brought up-to-date on China. Newspapers, universities, states, and flora all come into the story. All are identifiably American. In a fashion reminiscent of James Michener in *Centennial*, the present-day United States is connected to the world's archaeological past. The United States is portrayed as the knowledge centre of the world. Of course, Canada does not exist in the story.

Even in those instances where Canada does exist, it does so only in the Canadian edition. The relationship between the Canadian and American editions, of course, works in only one direction. The NFB film "A Day at the Calgary Zoo" is listed in the Canadian teacher's guide,[17] for example, but does not show up at all in the American edition.

These and other numerous examples to be found throughout *Reading 360* can only lead to the conclusion that, in short, the "Canadianization" process is a fraud. The literary quality of the material drops; factual precision is replaced with vagueness; American content remains predominant; and overall, an American point of view and pride of place still prevails.

Recent Developments in Reading Series

The reading series discussed above are all currently in use in many Canadian schools. However, all have been or are soon to be revised and therefore will soon be replaced. To illustrate the flavor of recent revisions, an examination was undertaken of *Starting Points (Revised)*[18] and Gage's *Expressways*[19] in the context of the foregoing analyses. A summary of that examination follows.

A few examples from the grade 6 books of *Starting Points* gives a sense of some of the problematic content. The first chapter of the first book begins with a lengthy fictional piece about baseball which has no explicit setting. However, it is plainly set in the United States, since reference is made to Jefferson High School and to "Coach Wilson," an American style of addressing such a person. This is followed by a short piece on "how baseball was brought to North America" which refers only to the United States. Two of the remaining three short pieces contain Canadian references and the chapter ends with another longer piece of fiction with only generic references. Another chapter begins with a fictional piece about an Indian girl on an island off the coast of California, and includes a poem entitled "Islands in Boston Harbour."

The second book also begins with a piece set in the United States, but with no explicit confining references. Its content, about some children vandalizing subways, harkens back to the individual persistence/hard knocks world of the original edition. As for the remainder of the book, generic references replace American references. The American references which remain are trivial. They are in connection with the development of the Frisbee, an U.S. history of roller skating (with some early references to other countries before it "took off" in the United States), and so forth.

In summary, in the first book 35 percent of the selections have Canadian content, in the second, 43 percent. Overall, the literary quality suffers as a result of the frequent use of two-page bits of information. Finally, the technique of excluding explicit American references from stories with obviously American settings provides for little faith in the respect of the editors-in-chief and publisher for Canadian cultural patterns and values.

Expressways presents quite a different picture. A tabulation of the longer prose selections in three of the six grades 4 to 6 books revealed that between 60 percent and 66 percent of the selections contain Canadian references. Few, in the order of 5 percent, refer to the United States, while approximately 25 percent have generic referents.

The distinguishing feature of *Expressways* is that while the themes of the Nelson series stand out as being typical and salient Canadian themes, most of *Expressways* is filled with tales of fantasy and adventure. The world presented is one of childhood bounded fairly much by the interests and amusements of the undirected consciousness of the child. While the geographical settings are explicitly Canadian, the imaginative universe is confined to the world of children with few cultural touchstones or undercurrents.

But whatever the shortcomings of the Gage program, it is interesting that this Canadian company has emphasized Canadian content more than has Ginn in *Starting Points*. The Gage program illustrates what ought to be the starting point for any program being used in Canada. It makes clear that the U.S.–Canada boundary need no longer be obscured as it is in *Starting Points* and has been even in previous series put out by Gage (see Figure 1.1).

Literature in Secondary Schools

It is relatively easy to get a fix on the pattern of content to which most elementary school children in Canada are exposed, because of the wide use of the kind of reading series which we have just discussed. In secondary school, however, we are faced with a different situation.

Here teachers no longer proceed selection-by-selection through the pages of the reader. In fact, although the days may be numbered for this practice by the extension of basal reading series into grades 7 and 8, teachers have been permitted to choose. They choose, in general, from provincially published lists of "approved selections."

The dominant elements of the curriculum in junior and senior high schools taken together are novels and book-length non-fiction. These are followed by drama, and then short stories and poetry. We have focussed upon those elements which receive the greatest emphasis.

No separation is made between junior and senior high materials because, in terms of Canadian content, differences are insignificant.

12

Novels and Book-Length Non-Fiction

In the eight provinces surveyed, 596 novels and book-length non-fiction works were found to be on provincial lists, approximately 120 of them authored by Canadians. Twenty-four novels were listed in five or more provinces, but of those, only five were Canadian. Ontario and Quebec were not included in this survey, Ontario because the list would have included almost every work listed in every other province, and Quebec because of the dominance of the French language and hence literature in French.

A look at Table 1.3 reveals that there are ten American authors, six British, five Canadian, and three from other countries to be found most frequently on provincial lists. That is quite an imbalance in Canadian content. Canadian material is available. Fully 120 Canadian novels are approved by the various provinces, but there appears to be no systematic or co-ordinated effort by provincial curriculum committees to make sure the most appropriate Canadian works are recommended to teachers.

Table 1.3 / Novels Most Frequently Listed as Available from or Recommended by Provincial Departments of Education

Title	Author	Nationality of Author	Number of Provinces Listed
To Kill a Mockingbird	H. Lee	American	8
The Pearl	J. E. Steinbeck	American	8
Lord of the Flies	W. Golding	British	8
Who Has Seen the Wind?	W. O. Mitchell	Canadian	7
The Old Man and the Sea	E. Hemingway	American	7
The Chrysalids	J. Wyndham	British	7
Animal Farm	G. Orwell	British	7
The Red Pony	J. Steinbeck	American	6
Pigman	P. Zindel	American	6
Great Expectations	C. Dickens	British	6
A Separate Peace	J. Knowles	American	6
Lost Horizon	J. Hilton	British	6
Lost in the Barrens	F. Mowat	Canadian	6
The Incredible Journey	S. Burnford	Canadian	6
The Mountain and the Valley	E. Buckler	Canadian	5
In the Heat of the Night	J. Bull	American	5
Shane	J. Shaefer	American	5
Cry, The Beloved Country	A. Paton	South African	5
Moonfleet	J. M. Falkner	British	5
The Grizzly	A. & E. Johnson	American	5
Kon-Tiki Expedition	T. Hyerdahl	Swedish	5
Never Cry Wolf	F. Mowat	Canadian	5
The Outsiders	S. E. Hinton	American	5
Anne Frank	A. Frank	Dutch	5

Table 1.4/Canadian Authored Novels Most Frequently Listed for Use by Provinces

Title	Author	Number of Provinces Listed
Who Has Seen the Wind?	W. O. Mitchell	7
Lost in the Barrens	F. Mowat	6
The Mountain and the Valley	E. Buckler	8
The Incredible Journey	S. Burnford	5
Never Cry Wolf	F. Mowat	5
Where Nests the Water Hen?	G. Roy	4
The Stone Angel	M. Laurence	4
More Joy in Heaven	M. Callaghan	4
Execution	C. McDougall	4
Each Man's Son	H. MacLennan	4
Barometer Rising	H. MacLennan	4
People of the Deer	F. Mowat	4
The Watch that Ends the Night	H. MacLennan	3
Death on the Ice	C. Brown and H. Horwood	3
Boss of the Namko Drive	P. St. Pierre	3
Leaven of Malice	R. Davies	3
Fifth Business	R. Davies	3
Two Solitudes	H. MacLennan	3
The Richman	H. Kreisel	2
The Loved and the Lost	M. Callaghan	2
Earth and High Heaven	G. Graham	2
A Jest of God	M. Laurence	2
Swamp Angel	E. Wilson	2
The Sacrifice	A. Wiseman	2
The White Eskimo	H. Horwood	2
Such Is My Beloved	M. Callaghan	2

The Seven Most Frequently Listed Novels in Canadian Secondary Schools

If Canadian literature is not being introduced in any systematic fashion, what is being introduced and how? Seven novels were listed in seven of the eight provinces whose lists we surveyed. Those novels, one might say, come closer to comprising the literary heritage of graduating Canadian school students than any other works. Interestingly, three were written by Americans, three by Englishmen, and one by a Canadian.

Before proceeding to the content of those works, three cautionary points should be made. Firstly, the analysis provided here is within the context of the question at hand, namely, to what degree does the curriculum present Canadian realities. Secondly, no argument is being made that all non-Canadian work should be removed from the curriculum. The exercise here is to show that the works most often listed by provinces centre upon three separate thematics representative of some of the central concerns of three different societies. Thirdly, if only because these works find their popularity in the adolescent market, no claim is being forwarded that these selections made by Canadian educators are representative of each nation's literature.

These Canadian, British, and American works, grouped by nationality, are very different from one another. Most significantly they are firmly tied to national concerns. But, being good literature, they explore these concerns in a way that can be appreciated beyond the national community. The question is: Do teachers introduce these works so students understand that they reflect different cultures? And, at the same time, are students introduced to a Canadian perspective? If such a perspective is introduced at all, it is certainly not given primary consideration if teachers follow the assumptions contained in the organization of the curriculum.

In the American works, *To Kill a Mockingbird*,[20] *The Pearl*, [21] and *The Old Man and the Sea*,[22] the tension between the individual and the social and natural world is played out. In the English works, *Lord of the Flies*,[23] *The Chrysalids*,[24] and *Animal Farm*,[25] the central concern is what can be expected when groups with certain characteristics gain power. The sole Canadian work, *Who Has Seen the Wind?*[26] is an exploration of the very basic styles of living and surviving during the 1930s. These works warrant a somewhat more detailed examination.

American ideology and the American Dream, as distinct from the American way of life, emphasize the decisions an individual comes to in making his or her way in the world. The hero, in making his deal with the social whole, is often seen as embodying a search for pan-cultural ideals such as "good" or "truth," beyond that which society as a whole has attained. Some form of sacrifice is inevitably called for, a sacrifice which confirms the hero's right to special status. In this way he appears somewhat superhuman and becomes a cultural leader, in fact the power figure in the American Dream.

This cluster of characteristics is present in the main characters of all three American works. Each novel focusses on the central character and builds a story around his actions and his conflicts with his environment. In *To Kill a Mockingbird*, a lawyer pits his will and oratory against a town determined to lynch a black man for the alleged rape of an outcast white woman. The force of a bigoted community is portrayed and contrasted to the force of the lawyer's justice and reason. The story of *The Old Man and the Sea* follows an old man in a small boat who catches a large fish. Rather than admit it is too large, he lets the fish pull him until it exhausts itself. He then sets course for home which is now out of sight. By the time he reaches land sharks have devastated his catch. The novel explores dogged tenacity carried beyond a fault to an inspiration. The tenacity is not a mere reaction, but a considered decision that shows the power of the individual will in a world full of those who simply sway with the ebb and flow of human affairs.

Steinbeck presents a much different type of character in *The Pearl*, but a character who nevertheless makes his individual arrangement with the social world. At the literal level, this short novel is a simple, poignant tale of a Mexican pearl diver and his family. The diver finds the pearl of his dreams, but the dream quickly becomes a nightmare that ends in thieving and tragedy. Much as in *To Kill a Mockingbird*, the social group and world are small and nasty yet terribly powerful. Faced with this given, characters need a strong individualism to come to terms with hard reality. *The Pearl* presents an alternative to absolute individualism by having the main character derive significant support from his family. But, as with the other books, the focus still remains with the struggle of the individual and with his rewards.

The English works offer a vivid contrast to these American novels. All three selections have Britain's World War II victory as an implicit backdrop. On the surface, *Animal Farm* tells the story of farm animals taking over the operation of the farm and the subsequent power struggles amongst the animals. *The Chrysalids* is an optimistic exploration, set in a post-nuclear world, of a group of young people with telepathic powers. The persecuted young annihilate their persecutors, creating an ethical dilemma. In *Lord of the Flies*, a group of public school boys, stranded on a desert island, are soon plunged into personality conflicts and barbarism by their terror.

At a deeper level, *Animal Farm* is a rather pessimistic exploration of class upheaval. *The Chrysalids* explores parallel issues of power in a world of genetically different generations. And *Lord of the Flies* is again a pessimistic exploration of the behavior of English schoolboys without their masters' imposed control.

The common element in these three books is "Who rules?" and "With what wisdom?" In some sense, all harken back to the trauma of Hitler. *Animal Farm* worries over how to deal with the socialists, the next stage in the social evolution that was confronting England even as Hitler's armies were being defeated. *Lord of the Flies* speculates on the socializing structures of English institutions and their ability to produce an elite capable of justice. *The Chrysalids* echoes with opposite, humanistic values, the Hitlerian concern for developing a super race.

Besides the different focus of concern between the American and British works, none of the three British novels has an individual at the centre of the tale. Small groups, bound together by a common set of interests, are the focus. The individual hero gives way to people-in-context, the psychological to the socio-political. Each explores a different facet of a major source of tension in British society. Each represents a thread in the fabric of British society. Individual vision is not put forward as the potential saving-grace, but differing beliefs affirmed by like-minded others are explored for what they can contribute to the social whole.

What then of the Canadian work? The characters in the sole Canadian work, *Who Has Seen the Wind?*, seem quite like single oaks standing against the horizon on a prairie rise. They are highlights in a vast, majestic, and unchanging landscape. The novel concerns a boy growing up in a small Saskatchewan town. Human beings are portrayed as engaged in ordinary but meaningful dramas. The time of the novel, the 1930s, is thematically Canadian. It was a time when people did little else but survive. The small, everyday, and immediate loom large insofar as it is these small lives, being doggedly repeated everywhere, that form the larger realities. Although focussed on individuals, there is also a strong social element. The characters emerge out of their land and conditions, time and place. They are neither American conquering heroes nor bound in with their British like-minded compatriots. They are Canadian. As Mitchell portrays them, they are not contrasted to the mass either as small group representatives or as representatives of some new ideology or capacity. They are, in fact, both separate individuals and mass representatives at the same time.

The above analysis suggests that it is not a distortion to point to the national similarities in, and international differences between, these "popular" works. These differences are major and are immediately obvious. They are the characteristics which have been recognized by the people of the author's country who have propelled the work to international status so the vision can be shared with people of other countries. However, the problem is that these works are not introduced to Canadian students as cultural artifacts. Rather they are introduced as pieces of "high quality" literature which all have something significant to offer the individual in his or her search to affirm a set of values. While this is undoubtedly true, the Canadian student is given no sense that his or her culture has its own particular set of values.

The Most Frequently Listed Canadian Works

Growing numbers of teachers have now had a systematic introduction to Canadian literature and other national literatures in university. As a result, they have at least some appreciation of the importance of the cultural context within which a writer works. Given the most frequently listed Canadian works, how might teachers with such training interpret those texts to point to special qualities of Canadian literature?

Table 1.4 presents the most frequently listed Canadian Works of fiction and non-fiction. The five most frequently listed can serve as a basis for our analysis. The most immediately noticeable similarity amongst these five — *Who Has Seen the Wind?*, *Lost in the Barrens*,[27] *The Mountain and the Valley*,[28] *The Incredible Journey*,[29] and *Never Cry Wolf*[30] — is that all have rural settings and that these settings play a large role in the resolution of the story's basic dilemma. The Prairies, the North, the Annapolis Valley, and northwestern Ontario are all vividly portrayed by the authors. In all but *The Mountain and the Valley*, nature is in some sense a protagonist. Accordingly, they all fit Atwood's characterization of Canadian literature as being centrally concerned with survival.

Two major elements are set forward in each. The first is how the varying individualities of each of the main characters serves the end of both survival and the creation of a life-style worthy of some contemplation. The second is the relation an individual has with both his immediate social unit, and, at times, with the greater social whole. Perhaps the romantic/real point of view developed by Mowat towards the wolves in *Never Cry Wolf* illustrates the point best. The story is a humorous account of the author's experience as a field biologist studying wolf behavior in the Keewatin Barrens. Along with his own close observation, Mowat presents his own set of myths about wolves as natural controls and of no danger to man. Not only does Mowat firmly place the wolf in his ecological niche, but he also provides the reader with some understanding of the manner in which a pack of wolves come to play out their role, both as predators and as cooperative hunters. The result is an interplay of three levels of definition. First is individual character; second, the immediate social or reference group; and third, the larger ecological or political context. These three levels are also developed in the other four works.

In *Lost in the Barrens*, Mowat also explores each level. Two boys, one Indian, one white, have become separated from their hunting party, and spend from fall to Christmas setting up a survival camp at the edge of the Northern treeline. Both characters have their own individuality. Both bring their cultural background to their situation. And both learn that nature can provide sustenance as well as be an immense power as an adversary.

In *Who Has Seen the Wind?*, all the characters appear to be drawn individually out of the earth to which they are so closely connected. Yet, all also have that second level of social background which gives them a set of assumptions which is basic to the way they meet their respective fates. *The Incredible Journey* has a strong flavor of a children's travelogue often found in British children's literature. Here the animals are the vehicle for a tour through the land and culture of northern Ontario. Although the basic theme, one which seems inevitable in pet stories, is the strength of the bond of a dependent relationship, the various characters the animals encounter on their journey illustrate a distinctive social milieu. Through such characters the author does indeed show the individual arrangement the people of this outback are making with the wilderness, and from what this arrangement is derived.

The Mountain and the Valley is a different kind of novel. It is not only not written specifically for adolescents, but its approach also plays nature and human beings against one another in quite a different manner than do the other novels. It is a character study of some residents of the Annapolis Valley, how they see the world and how they live out their lives. In fact, Buckler concentrates on the characters' interior lives. But his landscape is so vivid the reader cannot help but see these interiors as representations of land and nature.

In short, in each of these works we are introduced to ordinary but distinctive people. At the same time physical realities are elevated to the symbolic. From within the context of this Canadian voice, Canadian places are made known and are imbued with the magic of the story.

Canadian vs. Foreign Literatures

The above Canadian works can be distinguished from the British and American works listed on both a concrete and a symbolic level. The artificial settings of *Animal Farm, The Chrysalids,* and *Lord of the Flies* contrast to the Canadian works which are so profoundly connected to their natural setting. Similarly, while the Canadian works are connected with the everyday, the foci of *The Old Man and the Sea* and *To Kill a Mockingbird* are dramatic and visionary, not really in touch with the warp and woof of everyday living. *The Pearl* does emphasize elements of a lived world, but places this reality within the fantasy of being catapulted into a Shangri-La.

A solid introduction to a Canadian perspective through Canadian literature would serve both cultural and educational values by providing a home foundation of lived experience and literary representation. That, in turn, could form the basis for an appreciation of the literature and form of other cultures, in this case, the United States and Britain.

The problem with the present literature program and its organization is that while students understand the literature of both British and American cultures, because Canada imports American realities through the media, and British realities through its constitutional and intellectual inheritance, they have no home foundation to help them place that literature in context. What is presented to school students amounts to a thrice divided imagination variously attracted by these three major imaginative currents. Because of the emphasis placed on these two foreign ideologies, lived experience and one's own literature become small and provincial, encouraging, because they must compete with two other powerful literatures and visions, not only a colonized mentality in our adolescents, but also the foundations for a continuing acceptance of that colonial status. The imagination is captured.

Other Forms of Literature at the Secondary Level

With such a syllabic organization in novels, it would be unreasonable to expect the study of other forms of literature to reflect a recognition of cultural identity. Indeed, reviews of provincial curriculum documents as well as individual texts show that in each of the categories of drama, poetry, and short prose the curriculum is organized without highlighting what is Canadian from what is not. Because drama is so emphasized in secondary schools, a systematic survey of offerings was conducted of the same provinces surveyed for use of novels and book-length non-fiction.

Drama

The Ecstacy of Rita Joe[31] is a Canadian play written by George Ryga and published by Talonbooks, a small literary publisher based in Vancouver. It has played to packed houses in all parts of Canada and has sold nearly 200,000 copies in two editions. It has been to the Edinburgh Festival and to the United States. It has even been made into a ballet. It tells the story of the destruction of an Indian woman named Rita Joe, a destruction within the white man's world that is so powerful it makes impossible any attempt to dismiss it as a particular tragedy avoidable by a particular means.

The power of *Rita Joe* emerges in large part from its exploration of a human tragedy fundamental to contemporary Canada. European settlement of Canada was in large extent a response to a bureaucratically defined opportunity, to name three examples, Clifford Sifton's courting of Eastern European peasants, the early penetration of the railway, and the early presence of the Royal North West Mounted Police. Settlers were led to believe that the government, especially in the West, had arranged things through treaties with the Indians. They had. Few confrontations arose between the races. But many Indians still figure as apparitions on the edges of the white man's civilization, silent witnesses to the inequities of that "arrangement."

Rita Joe speaks to this disturbance of Canadian society and of the white Canadian mind. It speaks Indian sharply to both Indians and Whites. It speaks within Canada to Canadians so that all the world can hear.

Of 230 works listed in eight provinces, *Rita Joe* was the only Canadian play we found listed in at least three of the eight provinces in our initial survey. Except for Shakespeare, the remainder of the plays on the list of works available or recommended in three or more provinces are a potpourri of American and English dramas, with the addition of some Ibsen. They are gripping, humorous, and fanciful. They are set within the class structure of Britain, the streets of New York, the roads of the American Midwest, and a Confederate family of the American South. Few have not been turned into feature films or television dramas. Few have not been hailed as contemporary masterpieces. There is little question of their quality and impact. They can indeed be enjoyed by adolescents. But when such plays are introduced within a context which does not include works by Canadians and about Canadian culture, they simply do not meet our nation's need to introduce our own literary and cultural heritage.

Thirteen Shakespearean plays are listed in more than three provinces. In fact, except for one play, *Cyrano de Bergerac*,[32] all grade 10 plays listed on three or more provincial lists were written by Shakespeare. While the value of Shakespeare cannot be denied, the emphasis on the study of his works in grade 10 is surely misplaced when Canadian content is completely ignored.

The plays which appear most consistently from province to province are those which explore the tensions between the individual and the family, the small group, or society-at-large. In the case of plays, this is done in a particular setting. The importance of setting is that the audience or reader comes to see something magical in the setting for the events. It becomes larger than life. It becomes identified as a place where profound issues of life are dealt with. Its people become prototypical — they act not in the small way that each of us sees ourselves doing, but rather with significance, at the various levels of human existence: the psychological, social, political, and so forth. In other words, they act through the eyes of the artist.

Recent Developments in Secondary Literature

As of the beginning of 1982, two contradictory trends in secondary literature were visible. On the one hand, following a concern for "literacy," some provinces were considering adopting extensions of basal anthologies into the junior high grades. On the other hand, following the concern central to this book, some provinces, districts, and boards were attempting to disseminate information on Canadian materials. Both efforts give some reason to be pessimistic.

Examination of five anthologies aimed at the secondary market — *Insight,*[33] *Reflections,*[34] *Dialogue,*[35] *Inside, Outside,*[36] and *Inquiry into Literature*[37] — shows three not to have gone beyond a token inclusion of Canadian-authored material and material about Canada. In MacMillan's *Dialogue,* 46 percent of the acknowledged selections are Canadian. However, the book was published in 1972. In *Inside, Outside,* an extension of *Language Patterns: Impressions,* 50 percent of the content is Canadian-authored.

Two significant projects should be noted with regard to efforts to encourage teachers to use more Canadian material. Some time before 1977 the Writers' Development Trust developed ten resource guides with the following titles: *Action/Adventure, North and Native Literature, Coming of Age in Canada, The Immigrant Experience, New Land/New Language, The Family in Canadian Literature, Social Realism,* and *Women in Canadian Literature.*[38] The guides listed all Canadian work available on these topics, gave annotations, and suggested appropriate grades in which they might be used.

Following these guides, the province of Manitoba compiled two bibliographies of its own entitled *In Search of Canadian Materials*[39] and *In Search of Free Canadian Materials.*[40] They distributed these to teachers, boards, and schools in the province. In addition, many copies have found their way into libraries and resource centres outside the province.

Neither of these two sets of teaching aids is well known to teachers or is used extensively in faculties of education. The fact, quite simply, is that teachers and their trainers have not been availing themselves of tools to identify Canadian materials appropriate to their subject and grade.

Summary

To recapitulate, there are six key points. In the elementary grades provincial curricula concentrate upon skills to the neglect of content on the learning material side of the equation. In grades 1 to 3 the simplified world of the primary reader does not include Canadian realities. In grades 4 to 6 many reading series, especially those adapted from foreign series, do not present Canadian content or a Canadian perspective. In secondary schools concern for the study of quality literature in provincial curricula relegates Canadian material to a distant second place. Frequently, chosen materials present powerful American and British, and from time to time Canadian, themes. But it is rare for these works to be introduced in their national contexts. Certainly the curricula do not require it. Finally, new trends hold little hope of a commitment by curriculum planners, textbook publishers, education professors, or teachers to Canadian literature as a high priority.

Footnotes

1. J. R. Linn et al., eds. *Language Patterns* (Toronto: Holt, Rinehart and Winston, 1970).
2. J. McInnes and E. Hearn, eds., *The Nelson Language Development Reading Program* (Toronto: Thos. Nelson & Sons, 1971).
3. R. Lorimer; M. Hill; M. Long; and B. McLellan, "Consider Content: An Analysis of Two 'Canadian' Language Arts Reading Series," *Interchange* 8(4), 1977-78, 64-77.
4. B. Moore and H. Hooper, eds., *Starting Points in Reading* (Toronto: Ginn, 1973).
5. R. Lorimer; J. Harkley; M. Long; and D. Tourell, "Your Canadian Reader," *Lighthouse*, 1978, 6-15.
6. G. Martell, "Canadian Content in Canadian Readers," cited in A. Kennedy and M. Simmons, *Where We Live: Teacher's Guidebook* (Toronto: James Lorimer, 1978), p. 15.
7. Office of the Director of Education, Toronto Board of Education, *Canadian Authorship of Reading Programs*, 22 January 1980.
8. R. Lorimer and M. Long, "Sex-Role Stereotyping in Elementary Readers," *Interchange* 10(2), 1979-80, 25-45.
9. "The Bully of Barkham Street," in Moore and Hooper, *Starting Points*, pp. 32-49.
10. M. Atwood, *Survival: A Thematic Guide to Canadian Literature* (Toronto: House of Anansi, 1972).
11. N. Frye, *The Bush Garden: Essays on the Canadian Imagination* (Toronto: House of Anansi, 1971).
12. E. Mandel, *Contexts of Canadian Criticism* (Chicago: University of Chicago Press, 1971)
13. "The Sun That Warms," in T. Clymer, ed., *Reading 360* (Cdn. edition), p. 133.
14. "The Sun That Warms," in T. Clymer, ed., *Reading 360* (U.S. edition), p. 130.
15. "All Sorts of Things," in T. Clymer, ed., *Reading 360* (both editions).

16. "The Sun That Warms," in T. Clymer, ed., *Reading 360* (Cdn. edition), p. 113.

17. Teacher's Guide to "The Sun That Warms," in T. Clymer, ed., *Reading 360* (Cdn. edition).

18. Bill Moore, ed., *Starting Points in Reading (Revised) C1* and *C2* (Toronto: Ginn, 1981).

19. E. A. Thorn and J. M. Irwin, eds., *Expressways: Chinook, Pingo, Handshakings* (Levels 8, 10, and 12) (Toronto: Gage, 1980).

20. H. Lee, *To Kill a Mockingbird* (Philadelphia: Lippincott, 1960).

21. J. Steinbeck, *The Pearl* (New York: Viking Press, 1947).

22. E. Hemingway, *The Old Man and the Sea* (New York: Scribners, 1967).

23. W. Golding, *Lord of the Flies* (New York: Coward-McCann, 1962).

24. J. Wyndham, *The Chrysalids* (Toronto: House of Grant, 1965).

25. G. Orwell, *Animal Farm* (Harmondsworth: Penguin, 1951).

26. W. O. Mitchell, *Who Has Seen the Wind?* (Toronto: Macmillan, 1947).

27. F. Mowat, *Lost in the Barrens* (Boston: Little Brown, 1956).

28. E. Buckler, *The Mountain and the Valley* (Ottawa: Carleton Library Series, McClelland & Stewart, 1961.

29. S. Burnford, *The Incredible Journey* (Boston: Little Brown, 1961).

30. F. Mowat, *Never Cry Wolf* (Toronto: McClelland & Stewart, 1963).

31. G. Ryga, *The Ecstacy of Rita Joe* (Vancouver: Talonbooks, 1970).

32. E. Rostrand, *Cyrano de Bergerac* (Toronto: Oxford University Press, 1975).

33. K. J. Weber and M. H. Tudor, eds., *Insight 1: A Practical Approach to Language Arts* (Toronto: Methuen, 1980).

34. J. B. Bell and E. W. Buxton, eds., *Reflections* (Toronto: Wiley, 1975).

35. H. M. Covell and J. W. Greig, eds., *Dialogue* (Toronto: Macmillan, 1972).

36. J. Booth, ed., *Impressions: Inside, Outside* (Toronto: Holt, Rinehart and Winston, 1978).

37. B. Fillion and J. Henderson, eds., *Inquiry into Literature 1* (Toronto: Collier Macmillan, 1980).

38. Writers' Development Trust, *Canadian Literature Resource Guides* (Toronto: Writers' Development Trust, 1977).

39. D. Phillips, ed., *In Search of Canadian Materials* (Winnipeg: Department of Education, 1978).

40. J. Pampallis, ed., *In Search of Free Canadian Materials* (Winnipeg: Department of Education, 1978).

2: Canadian Content and a Canadian Perspective in Social Studies

Introduction

The social studies curriculum is organized on somewhat different principles than those which shape language arts. Social studies begins with a concern for *content*; that is, social, historical, or geographical information. Course content is apparent in such titles as "Families," "Community," "Canada in her North American Setting," or "Ancient Civilizations."

As a subject, social studies interprets this information to provide students with a social context for living through understanding their community and culture.

Over the past few decades, however, social studies has also emphasized active inquiry or "engagement." Active inquiry or engagement is the ability to *inquire* into social phenomena and to make judgments about what might be considered best, based on *values* to which one adheres. These judgments are intended to serve as a basis for action. Taken to a further level of abstraction, one can even inquire into and judge one's own values. The basic idea, one which derives from Piagetian thinking, is that social and moral judgments and abilities increase in complexity and sophistication just as do mathematical judgments and abilities.

The focus of our examination of social studies is to determine what and how much Canadian content is presented to students and, secondly, how that content is treated. That task includes assessing the roles of "inquiry" and "values" in determining both content and treatment of content. For instance, if a curriculum builds from the self and family through the neighborhood to the region, and subsequently to the nation, to the civilization, and then to the world, a profound Canadian viewpoint can be developed. But if course materials tell the story of Canada by continually basing discussion on developments in the United States, they can foster a profound American focus and a tacit Canadian colonial mentality. Similarly, if a program emphasizes values and/or the process of inquiry to the neglect of content, then the importance of Canadian information is underplayed.

This chapter will concentrate on provincial curriculum guidelines and learning materials for what they reveal about content and its treatment.

The Elementary Social Studies Curriculum

Because each province has its own system of naming courses, it is difficult to present an overall picture of elementary social studies. Even then the picture is continually in flux because, at any one time, at least one province will be revising its curriculum. Decentralized decision-making, especially in Ontario, increases the difficulties of presenting a national picture even further.

In spite of the above difficulties, several years ago Nova Scotia social studies consultant, Glenda Redden, provided a chart and considerable other information about the social studies curriculum across Canada for the Council of Ministers of Education, Canada (CMEC).[1] That chart is updated here and presents the current picture of what provinces are doing in elementary social studies.

As the chart indicates, provincial elementary curricula are most commonly based on the notion of "expanding horizons" in both a geographic and conceptual sense of the term. This notion means that teaching programs base comment and learning upon the experience, knowledge, and capabilities of the child. Through discussion and the introduction of new information, the curriculum expands upon that experience and uses it as a touchstone for the exploration of ever expanding horizons.

An Overview of the Elementary Curriculum

In general in kindergarten/primary, children are introduced to stimulating activities but within the concrete social context of their own neighborhoods. These activities are intended to give children a sense of themselves as individuals in the social world.

In grade 1, the family is the central focus for comment. In one program, pictures of families in various settings are provided to stimulate discussion. There is a wedding in Vancouver, a refugee family in Zaire, three generations of an English family gathered to celebrate Christmas, and so forth. The family is introduced in its myriad forms to give children insight into the fragmentary patterns of family life they see everyday.

In grade 2, the activities of people, and the organization of these activities, serves to introduce communities. Typical examples in the same program are the central core of Paris, a sheep station in New Zealand, a small town in Manitoba, and an Inuit village. This material provides a base for the grade 3 program, a comparative and more intensive analysis of families and communities.

Provincial Social Studies Curricula, k-12 (13), 1982

	British Columbia	Alberta	Saskatchewan	Manitoba	Ontario
K				Exploring My World	k-6 to acquaint children with their social and scientific environment both in some of its specifics and as a whole pattern
1	Families (local)	Families	Families (Task Force just reported to Minister)	Human needs and Interdependence	
2	Communities B.C.	Neighborhood Cdn Communities	Communities	Changes	– to help children acquire the info & skills they need to live in a multicultural society – to build foundations for informed rational attitudes and decisions
3	Interaction of Communities (Canada)	Life Styles in times & places (Cdn oriented)	Cities	Communities Today	– to use enthusiasm generated by active investigation to stimulate other aspects of learning
4	Early Settlement in Canada (Natives Explorers)	Alberta — our province	Province of Saskatchewan	Communities around the world	– to lead to a reasoned knowledge and pride in Canada

5	Development of Canada: Settlement, Gov't, Later Immigration	Canada — our people	Canada	Life in Canada Today: regional orientation	
6	The World Community: Four Peoples from Four Continents	Meeting human needs: past, far east, civics	Americas — our hemisphere	Life in Canada's Past	
7	People & Places: Can. present, past, pre-contact & European settlement; world present, south temperate climate, mediterranean climate, past B.C.	People & their Culture: indiv. & society; non-industrial society; Can. multicultural society.	Geography of Eastern Europe	Spaceship Earth	*History:* Story of Canada & Canadians *Geography:* North & South American Continents
8	Our Diverse Heritage (Geography plus Middle Ages in Europe, Middle East, and Orient; Renaissance & Reformation in Europe; Exploration & Conquest; Current developments.)	People & their Institutions: Can. political institutions; Can. individual & institutions; nation & citizen: Asia & Africa	Canada's Heritage	People Through the Ages	*History:* Story of Canada & Canadians *Geography:* North & South American Continents
9	No Title (N. American geography, European settlements to 1815; Nation building; Europe, North America & elsewhere;	People & their Technology: people & industrial growth; gov't & human freedoms; Introd. of new technologies	Origins of Western Civilization	Canada Today/Canadian Studies	*History:* Contemporary Canada & World Concerns *Geography:* Canada

Industrialization Europe & North America; Current developments.)				
10 No Title (Confederation: causes & consequences ; Development of west; Canada's resources & industries; Canada & the Pacific; Current developments.)	Participatory Citizenship: human rights in Can.; Can. unity; Canada & the world	S.S.: Man the Individual / *History:* Middle Ages to 1848 / *Geog.:* Physical & Cultural	North America: a geographical perspective (1983)	*History:* Contemporary Canada & World Concerns or Canada's Multicultural Heritage / *Geography:* Europe & Asia
11 No Title (Government organizaton & power, emphasis on Canada; 20th century & Canada; Global resources, geography & economic study, emphasizing 1st and 3rd worlds.)	Global Issues: patterns of change; population & resource distribution	S.S.: Cross cultural comparisons / *History:* Contemp. World – 1848-Pres. / *Geog:* N. America / *Economics* / *Psychology*	Canadian Historical Perspectives	*History:* Ancient & Medieval World / *Geography:* Studies in Physical Geography: human, regional, urban
12 *Western Civilization Modern World Problems Intro to Discipline of Geography*	Global Issues: political & economic systems also, numerous social science & social issues options	S.S.: Canadian Studies / *History:* Canadian History / *Geography:* Populations / *Economics:* Canadian Perspectives / *Psychology*	World Issues	*History:* Origins of the Modern World / *Geography:* Studies in Physical Geography: human, regional, urban

Provincial Social Studies Curricula k-12 (13), 1982

	Newfoundland	Prince Edward Island	Nova Scotia	New Brunswick*	Quebec
13	*History:* Canadian, or U.S. or Canadian/U.S. *Geography:* Canadian Geographic realities or World Issues in Geographical Interpretation				
10-12	Canadian Economics Man in Society Law Consumer Studies World Religions				
K	K-Immediate Environment		P: Orientation to Self, School, Family & Neighborhood		
1	Living Together in Home, School & Neighborhood	Child, Farm, School, Neighborhood	Families	*Seven Strands* (through all grades): 1. understanding behavior — self & others (*individuals*)	Local Environment: home, family, classroom

2	Local Environment	2. *group* process to develop human relations, responsibility & empathy	Community/Communities	Neighbourhood – Communities: rural/urban	Local Community
3	Region	3. acquiring knowledge & appreciation of *local communities*	Canadian Communities	Local Communities	Meeting Needs of Communities: Nfld & Labrador
4	Geography of Quebec/ Pioneers of New France/Distant Localities	4. environmental awareness 5. values & valuing	People & their Changing Environment	Selected Canadian & World Communities	Canadian & World Communities
5	Transportation: sea, rail/Life in New France; Fall of New France	6. understanding democracy	Canada & the World's Peoples	Scandinavia/U.K./France	Our Province: Newfoundland & Labrador
6	Transportation: air/ Americas/earth, moon, fur, lumber	7. international relations	Nova Scotia (Atlantic Canada)	Prince Edward Island (Atlantic Canada)	Our Country: Canada
7	Introduction to Geography	Western Hemisphere	Pre-Confederation Canadian History/ Canadian Geography/ Civics (Local gov't)	*History:* Canadian to 1814 *Geog.:* Regional Can.	*History:* World – early civilizations to middle ages *Geog.:* Introduction to World Geography I
8	Introduction to History (Quebec examples)	History & Geography of Canada	Post-Confederation Canada/N.America Geography/Civics (Provincial gov't)	*History:* Canada, 1814-1900 & Civics *Geography:* British Isles & Germany	*History:* World History – 16th-20th centuries *Geography:* Introduc-

Grade						
9	tion to World Geography II	*History:* Our Canadian Heritage *Geography:* Canadian geography — interdependence	*History:* Canada, 1900-Present & Civics	British History/European Geography/Civics (Federal gov't)	Establishing a World View	*History:* Evolution of the Modern World in Europe & USSR *Geography:* World Regions
10		***Reorganized High School Prog.* Core: Newfoundland Culture Democracy Canadian Studies: Canadian Economy Canadian Issues Canadian Law	*History:* Ancient & Medieval *Geog.:* Developing World *Gen. Hist.:* Canadian Studies *Gen. Geog.:* Canada	*History:* Ancient & Medieval *Geog.:* Environmental *S.S.:* Canada Studies	*History:* Ancient & Medieval *Geog.:* Physical *S.S.:* Canadian Studies & 20th Century	*History:* New France; Canada/Quebec *Geography:* Canada & Quebec
11		World Studies World Geog. (Human) World Problems Modern World History Alternative World Studies	*History:* Mod. World *Geog.:* Our Changing World *Gen. Hist.:* World Survey I *Gen. Geog.:* World	*History:* Western Europe *History:* 20th C. World *Geog.:* Canada *Canadian Economics*	*History:* Modern Hist. *Geog.:* Physical *S.S.:* Canadian Issues	*History:* Contemporary World *History:* Civilization of Classical Antiquity *Geog.:* Great Powers & International Exchanges *Geog.:* Physical & Human Geography *Economics:* Intro to Family & Consumer

History: Canada
Geog.: Canada
S.S.: World Problems
Economics
Political Science

*History: U.S./Cdn.
Geog.: Settlement
Geography
Gen. Hist.: Canada
National & Internat-
ional Economics
Modern World Prob-
lems
Political Science
Law
Sociology*

*History: Canadian
Survey & Civics
Geog.: Introductory
Economic Geography
Gen. Hist.: World
Survey II
World Problems
Introductory Econo-
mics
Introductory Politics
Advanced Politics
Consumer Economics
Introductory Law
P.E.I. History*

Electives:
Nfld Economic
Geography
U.S. History
Industry, Technology
& Society
Career Education

*New Brunswick is to introduce a history of New Brunswick at Grade 5 level (with a new text) in 1984

**Based on Reorganization Report August, 1979

12

Such a sequence of activities and information in the first three and a half grades encourages children to extend their understandings to parallel situations in the broader political community in which they live. With this understanding of the formation and context of communities, the major attributes of Canada's regions and national identity can successfully be introduced. At the regional level, cultural and economic patterns that result from personal contact, local geography, ethnic background, and common working occupations all provide a basis not only for discussion but also for an outline of possible future occupational opportunities and restrictions which these children will confront.

This extension is developed in grades 4, 5, and 6 by the introduction of other concrete dimensions, including political, historical, and geographic facts which have dictated the boundaries of region and nation. This material not only consolidates their basis of understanding, but also provides them with a sense of the larger national and international community within which they live.

Six and a half years of expanding upon the experience, knowledge, specific social background, and regional identity of Canadian children lays a firm foundation for self-understandings as well as understandings of the concepts of family, neighborhood, community, region, country, and world community.

A Province-by-Province Analysis

All provinces roughly follow such a sequence of expanding horizons in their curriculum. Alberta, Saskatchewan, and Newfoundland do so most closely. Those provinces that are less strict in their adherence to this sequence often introduce content conceptually at odds with any systematic exploration of the social world. Most often, also, that content is not Canadian. British Columbia neglects the provincial region in favor of a study of natives and explorers. Manitoba also neglects the provincial region, to a degree, and introduces the study of world communities at the grade 4 level before discussing Canadian communities. After initially using an expanding curriculum from kindergarten to grade 3, Nova Scotia moves to a worldwide scope. People and their changing environments are discussed in grade 4, while Canada and the world's peoples are the focus in grade 5. Then in grade 6, Nova Scotia and the Atlantic region is discussed.

In Prince Edward Island, the curriculum broadens in orderly fashion until grade 4, at which point a comparative dimension between Canadian and world communities is introduced. This is followed in grade 5 by a course centring on the U.K., France, and Scandinavia. At the grade 6 level, the provincial region is introduced, and then the national dimension is examined in the form of Canadian geography and history in junior high.

In Quebec, expanding horizons are introduced and they are also tied together with binding themes. Family is explored in grade 1, along with four other major related attributes, under the title of *"Temps, Durée, Espace, Habitat, Famille."* The social and physical orientation on the local environment of grade 1 is deepened and humanized in grade 2. Under the titles *"Les Hommes et les Choses Autrefois"* and *"Les Services et les Besoins Fondamentaux,"* the "beginnings of things" which surround the child are explored. The needs of human beings and how they are met within urban society are given specific focus in grade 3 as neighborhood and region are explored through an emphasis on *"Habitat et Architecture — Moyens de Transport et Systeme Routier — Aspects Historique de la Region."* In grade 4, the province is explored further in historical focus. The human geography and the pioneering of New France are discussed and contrasted with those of distant localities. In grade 5, the historical dimension remains, while grade 6 students explore both fur and timber staples and the earth and the moon. Canada as a separate subject of study and as distinct from Quebec is not introduced into the elementary curriculum.

In Ontario and New Brunswick the curricula have the appearance of being very different. The Ontario provincial guidelines do little more than list the following goals: to acquaint children with their social and scientific environment in some of its specifics and as a whole pattern; to help children acquire the information and skills they need to live in a multicultural society; to build foundations for informed, rational attitudes and discussions; to use the enthusiasm generated by active investigation to stimulate other aspects of learning; and to lead to a reasoned knowledge and pride in Canada. Individual school boards and teachers must turn these goals into courses. However different such an approach may seem, the resulting programs turn out to be much the same.

New Brunswick formulates its curriculum in terms of "seven strands"* of content throughout all six grades. They are: developing self-understanding and a knowledge of human behavior; using the group process to develop good human relations, respect, and empathy; acquiring a knowledge and appreciation of the local and regional communities; restoring and maintaining the quality of the total environment of man; clarifying values and understanding the process of valuing; understanding the democratic process; and gaining perspectives on international relations. These strands, on closer examination, prove to be not much more than different names for introducing the same content as do the other provinces. But they do ensure that the national dimension is introduced in New Brunswick only in the context of international relations and/or the democratic process. Canadian information is not a strand to be explored in and of itself.

---

*The above strands discussed here are descriptive of the Anglophone curriculum in New Brunswick.

Curriculum Assessment — Elementary

The guiding philosophy behind the "expanding horizons" curriculum is fairly self-evident. Children bring to new phenomena an understanding based on personal or lived experience. As they get older and gain linguistic facility, this personal experience also includes what they are told or what they have read. The implication is that new phenomena introduced to children should be related to their personal experience. As these new phenomena are comprehended, the children expand their breadth and depth of understanding on the basis of successively more divergent examples. This does not imply that children cannot understand examples far afield of their own experience, but rather that a richness of understanding can be built up through successively more different and distant examples.

The design of the curriculum, discounting each province's individual set of diversions from the basic expanding horizons plan, is sound. However, the application of the expanding horizons approach has not guaranteed the inclusion of Canadian content. In simple terms this is because the individual, the family, the community, and the world can all be introduced in generic form. Only does the generic becomes next to impossible when region and nation are discussed. Squeezed between generic portrayals of all other aspects of social life, as is done for example in McGraw-Hill's *Social and Environmental Series,*[2] the amount of concrete Canadian information which is introduced can indeed be paltry. The lack of Canadian content is limited further by the failure, until very recently, of provincial curricular documents to insist upon the use of concrete Canadian examples to fill out the learning materials recommended.

Within the past half decade several provinces, such as Alberta[3] and Ontario,[4] have begun to correct this inadequacy and to specify the necessity of the inclusion of Canadian content. Indeed, only in New Brunswick is movement towards Canadianization, beyond a commissioned provincial history for the grade 5 level, difficult to see. What remain problematical in the present elementary curricula are the interruptions, omissions, reversals, and incompletions of an orderly expansion of horizons, anomalies which are present in B.C., Manitoba, Quebec, Nova Scotia, P.E.I., and Newfoundland. They are not justified anywhere in provincial curriculum documents. Interruptions overemphasize the importance of face-to-face dynamics as determinants of social, political, and cultural interchange. Omissions, usually of the region, reflect an effort to induce a pan-regional perspective, something which may encourage mobility from provinces whose economics are marginal. Incompletions neglect the national dimension.

The alternative to curricula with such anomalies is to adopt a logically sequenced, straightforward expanding horizons curriculum infused with Canadian content. Such a curriculum introduces the student step-by-step to the various levels of social interaction starting with individuals, continuing through various levels of community to the nation, and ending with international and intercultural exchanges in the world. Its organizing principle is that a person's identity is wrapped up in all levels of social relationships, from the face-to-face through informal social relations to relations engendered by formal political and cultural institutions. The organization of the curriculum in accordance with this principle affirms all aspects of social life, including the interpersonal, the small group, the communal, the political, the economic, and the cultural. Thereby it underlines the multi-tiered nature of social identity. Such a curriculum does not shy away from the description of differences between the uniqueness of individuals, which begin in family and community, perhaps even in biology, and flower in the region and nation. Nor does it hide aspects of a person's identity which both forge allegiances and erect barriers between people of other regions and nations. Simply speaking, it builds and broadens notions of self, others, and societies and the interlinkages between them at all levels of social interaction.

Elementary Social Studies Learning Materials

Teachers and learning materials implement the design of the curriculum. Here the role of learning materials will be the focus of attention. A later chapter will discuss the influence of teachers on curriculum implementation.

Learning materials are a weaker force in elementary social studies than they are in elementary language arts. For example, one recent study[5] reports that expenditures on social studies learning materials in the elementary grades in Nova Scotia were 11.23 percent of the total learning materials budget, compared to 44.8 percent in language arts. Part of the reason for this low level of expenditure is that children's limited reading abilities often mean that teachers will utilize other media such as pictures, films, slides, or cassettes. But even these resources are often not used extensively in a manner consistent with the logic of their design. An informal survey of the use made of the Fitzhenry and Whiteside social studies Study Prints, *One World* [6] has shown that teachers used the materials infrequently and most often as convenient illustrations for their own structured lesson and course.[7] But this does not mean that we can afford to ignore the design and content of such materials. At the very least, they show the intentions of social studies experts and provincial authorities. And, used or not, they provide a framework within which social studies is carried on in the elementary grades.

The widely used Fitzhenry and Whiteside program will be presented as an in-depth example. Two other programs will be introduced in the following "assessment" section.

One World introduces considerable variety on a thoroughly Canadian base of families and communities. Everyday happenings — the father kissing his daughter-bride, the mail carrier, the adult controlling the amount of television watched, the Pakistani-Vancouverites celebrating — are all illustrated by Canadian pictures. None of the photos offers some clever visual clue to identify it as "peculiarly Canadian." Rather, on the reverse side of the picture, the location at which they were photographed is identified. By using this simple technique, Canadian content ceases to be a special case or a forced situation. Industrial, business, and cultural shots such as the CNR switching yards, the Vancouver Airport, the oil operations at Leduc, the totem poles at Skidegate, Toronto City Hall, and an Inuit church service, combine to give a sense of the fabric and dynamism of Canadian culture. Remnants of notions of being second class, not quite as advanced, or somewhat of a backwater, the kinds of feelings that come from seeing photos of the American-owned *Manhattan* crossing the Arctic, the U.S. submarine *Nautilus* reaching the North Pole under water, or the first American moon landings, all of which can be found in other current reading series, are banished.

The series also emphasizes regional content within a broader national perspective. In the set I have examined, 56 of the 96 pictures in the year one material are Canadian and 26 of those are set in British Columbia. In year two, 63 of the 95 pictures are Canadian, 47 of those British Columbian. In year three, 20 of the 50 pictures are set in Canada, 9 in British Columbia. In short, British Columbia students receive what appears to be a solid regional and national perspective within a world context.

The rest of the world is represented by a considerable variety of non-Canadian content. Table 2.1 shows the Third World as the dominant category, with Western Europe and the United States a distant second. Eastern Europe, including the U.S.S.R., is entirely unrepresented.

Learning Materials Assessment — Elementary

A world view can be extrapolated from the distribution of the Fitzhenry and Whiteside pictures. To begin with, the material is present- and future-oriented. In the sense that rich, developed nations are having to realign themselves with poor nations, it is probably a good thing for children to get an early understanding that there are many people in the world who live under much harsher economic and social circumstances than Canadians. The introduction of Third World material provides that context.

But a primary emphasis on the Third World, brought about by its being the most frequent foreign category, presents a number of problems. First, it excludes Europe and especially the founding cultures of Canada — the British, the French, and the Amerindians — thus creating an ahistorical viewpoint. It fails to give children a sense that our culture has developed from others and that we share a basic world view and life-style with other nations of the developed world. Without an understanding of our cultural and institutional roots an isolationist perspective is difficult to avoid. Look-

Table 2.1 / The Geographical Location of Families and Communities Portrayed in a Grades 1 to 3 Social Studies Series Published by Fitzhenry and Whiteside

Geographical Location	Frequency of Occurrence		
	Grade 1	Grade 2	Grade 3
Canada:	56	63	20
British Columbia	26	47	9
Past	10	13	0
Europe:	5	6	12
Great Britain	3	2	5
France	0	1	0
United States:	6	2	7
Third World:	29	21	11
Africa/India/Asia	14	14	6
South America	3	2	1
Australia	1	3	2
China	0	2	2
U.S.S.R.:	0	0	0
Eastern Europe:	0	0	0
TOTALS	96	95*	49**

*The grades 2 and 3 sets available to this study were incomplete.
**In grade 3, multiple pictures from different countries occurred on the fronts of some of the cards. On the backs, from time to time were even more countries. Only the fronts were tabulated.

ing to domestic affairs, the world of *One World* provides little foundation for a person to grasp a sense of the major cultural differences within the country, especially between the French and the British, and the Native.

Second, the total lack of mention of any Eastern European countries or the U.S.S.R. not only completely ignores the major contribution Eastern Europeans have made to the country (Ukranians being the most obvious example), but also it ignores the political realities of Canada, past and present. Experiments with the social democracy characteristic of modern Eastern Europe are a vibrant and accepted part of political life in Canada.

The emphasis on British Columbia also limits the usefulness of the series for other provinces. Although the series is used in Ontario, New Brunswick, and Nova Scotia, the publisher has made no attempt to provide alternative editions for these provinces.

Third and last, with material from well over a dozen countries with vastly different cultures as well as material from Canada past and present, the variety of material may overwhelm the students, not to mention the teacher's ability to make such material meaningful to the students. Manitoba is often as foreign as Madagascar to British Columbia children at this level. When Manitoba is introduced through historical photos, the people look more like the Aymara Indians of Bolivia than contemporary Canadians. It should be remembered that grade 1 pupils think in simple dichotomies. They have little notion of countries, provinces, cities, and their hierarchical relations. As a consequence, the Fitzhenry and Whiteside program may undermine the formation of concepts within which children organize and assimilate information about people.

Whatever its shortcomings, however, this program provides an extensive introduction to Canadian culture *per se*, especially suited to British Columbians. Such content in turn serves as an appropriate backdrop to the development of an understanding of other cultures of the world. The same cannot be said of another series in fairly widespread use — McGraw-Hill's *Social and Environmental Studies (SES)* program. This program is essentially a transmutation of a language arts approach complete with focal emphasis on "scope and sequence" and skill development. Level One introduces the world of the individual in the abstract. Level Two introduces *Beaver Hill*, the prototypical generic community outlined in the previous chapter on language arts. Level Three diverges into Canadian content with concentration on large Canadian cities, Quebec and Newfoundland, and the Prairies. In Levels Four, Five, and Six, the program swings back to the global village, the eastern hemisphere and the western hemisphere respectively. In these latter three levels, only two of the twenty-seven topics covered have Canadian content. It is not accidental that only one year (i.e., one-sixth) of this program needs to be changed as it is marketed through the worldwide offices of McGraw-Hill.

A more recent program published by Gage, *Canada: Our Roots and Environment*,[8] falls midway between *One World* and the *SES* program. The program covers grades 3 to 6, and in terms of Canadian content, falls fairly much in line with Fitzhenry and Whiteside's *One World*. The topics in grade order are *Canada: Our Home, Canada: Our People, Canada: Our Heritage,* and *Canada: Our Place in the World.* Compared to *One World*, the materials provide a more comprehensive exploration of the content they present. However, diversity is only geographic. The multicultural and multifaceted nature of our society is only indirectly covered through the examination of many of the countries from which Canadians have emigrated.

Social Studies in Junior High — The Curriculum

In 1979 things looked bleak in junior high curricula with regard to Canadian content, especially in western Canada. Only one course in all the western provinces, Saskatchewan's "Canada's Heritage," was directly oriented to Canada. The others were concerned with various topics such as ancient civilizations, the geography of the eastern hemisphere, culture and technology, and cultural stages. While historians, geographers, and anthropologists could undoubtedly explain the relevance of these courses to Canada, few teachers and fewer students were aware of such connections. There was also increasing movement in the west to courses emphasizing inquiry and values, and hence, engagement.

In the east, the situation was quite different but no more heartening. Ontario, Quebec, New Brunswick, Nova Scotia, and Prince Edward Island taught a dual Canadian history/geography in grades 7 and 8. Newfoundland children examined Newfoundland, North American neighborhoods, the world and Canadian heritages. However, partly as a result of dated and flawed materials, commitment to these Canadian-oriented courses was flagging.

In the first part of this section we will review those courses oriented to inquiry and engagement and contrast them to very recent revisions which are taking junior high social studies in a Canadian direction. Then we will contrast the older materials used predominantly in the east with newer ones to demonstrate a resurgence of commitment to Canadian-oriented courses in that region.

Although recent revisions have curtailed an emphasis on inquiry and engagement, the approach has far from disappeared from the curriculum and retains many adherents amongst teachers. A review of its characteristics is useful. The clearest example of the approach is contained in an Alberta Education document entitled *Experiences in Decision-Making* [9] which, until the Fall of 1982, served Alberta's teachers as a curriculum outline. The program began in grades 7, 8, and 9 with a swirl of courses oriented around "Man, Technology and Culture." By focussing elsewhere within a framework of ideals and values, the students were shown the imperfections in the realities of other societies and the strengths of the ideals of contemporary Western society. In one course called "Pre-Industrial Society," students examined three themes: "What is Man?," "What is Culture?," and "What is Technology?" Each theme had several "value issues" to orient the discussion. Under the third theme, for example, the two values issues identified were: (1) "To what extent has technological change benefitted pre-industrial societies?"; and (2) "Should a pre-industrial society do what is technically possible, whether or not it is socially desirable?"

Another course, "Afro-Asian Society," focussed on four value issues: (1) "Should individual worth be maximized in an Afro-Asian Society?"; (2) "Should Afro-Asian societies change the methods by which resources are utilized?"; (3) "Should social and cultural change in an Afro-Asian society be viewed as necessary and desirable?"; and (4) "Should an Afro-Asian society pursue a policy of non-alignment?" In the course on "Western Society," students were asked: (1) "How should the society under study resolve conflicts between individual freedom and group control?"; (2) "How should Western societies use technology to achieve the goals of mankind?"; and (3) "How should individuals and social groups of differing political, economic, social and cultural convictions adjust so as to minimize conflicts with the Western world?"

While the wisdom of a curriculum with such an apparent naiveté and ethnocentricism is questionable, the important consideration for this discussion is how such courses contribute to the development of a Canadian perspective, since certainly they have no Canadian content to speak of. The placement of the content of these courses within a value perspective, as the orienting themes and issues suggest, is a powerful device which encourages a vague allegiance to "the way we do things" and hence to the social priorities inherent in Western society. It does so by asking questions which make sense within our culture's values and ideas. But what sense can junior high school students make of the question: "Should individual worth be maximized in an Afro-Asian society?" The question, barely more than rhetorical, takes our cultural viewpoint and asks a group of young teenagers if Afro-Asian society is ready to receive a watered-down version of our civilization.

Such a curriculum design recognizes the concern of young adolescents who are forming their first social allegiances. But, by looking elsewhere, and then turning to "home" at a level of ideals, it encourages the development of an allegiance that cannot stand up to examination as students take a more inquisitive approach to their own values and society. For instance, there is no information in these courses about the formal and informal means which allow Canada to function in a relatively democratic and just way, and what constitutes its major tensions and problems. Mechanisms that help us achieve our ideals — wealth redistribution schemes between provinces, government monopolies in the form of crown corporations in utilities, government support for the arts, medicare, a political climate which encourages entrepreneurial activities both in the private and public sector, tariffs, regulatory agencies — are not introduced. Their existence and purpose are not described, so they cannot be scrutinized and understood more completely as the students mature.

The Present Situation: The New Junior High Curricula

With the publication of the Downey Report[10] in 1975, the Alberta government was becoming aware of at least some of these problems. By 1981, it, like many other provinces, had begun to take remedial steps.*

---

*A Saskatchewan ministerial task force on Social Studies K-12 recommended in mid-December 1981 a major revision of the social studies curriculum. Included in its suggestions for revision was a recommendation to strengthen the Canadian component of the curriculum.

Social studies at the junior high level has changed immensely over the past three years, especially in Alberta and British Columbia, but also in Manitoba.[11] Under considerable pressure, usually from outside the education community, these provinces have introduced Canadian content. They have brought the content of their courses in line with most of the eastern provinces such as Ontario, Prince Edward Island, and to some extent, Nova Scotia and Quebec. The change on a national scale has been dramatic.

In all provinces at the junior high level in 1977-79, in total six courses offered partial Canadian content and a further six were wholly devoted to the study of Canada. Today, fully eighteen courses at the junior high level are either wholly devoted to the study of Canada or have Canadian information as a basis for comparative study. Two other courses, in Quebec, use Canadian examples in their discussion of the disciplines of geography and history.

The dramatic nature of the change is evident in two provincial charts. The first illustrates the direction Alberta has taken.[12] As columns one and three show, values and skills still play a major part in the Alberta curriculum, but they are now focussed on concrete content, i.e., "knowledge objectives." If, as the ministry now claims in its curriculum guidelines, approximately 60 percent of the social studies curriculum is Canadian, such changes represent a profound reorientation. However, that level of Canadian content has not been achieved purely through curriculum revision. The Alberta government has spent the large sum of $8.38 million of Heritage Fund money to develop Canadian, western Canadian, and Alberta-oriented materials for all grades. Twelve multi-media kits, called the *Kanata Kits*, were prepared specifically for social studies. Four were specifically designed for the junior high level. (Much of the other money was spent on providing Canadian literature for all levels of the curriculum.)

The second chart is a composite of a British Columbia government draft document written in 1980 and partially implemented in a slightly revised form in September 1983.[13] The revisions reflect not only a basic change of philosophy but also the inclusion of explicit Canadian material at nearly every level in the, presumably final, 1984 revision. Column 1 describes the existing curriculum with its far-ranging explorations of cultural history, developing countries, the renaissance, industrialization, Canada in a continental context, and contemporary world issues. Column 2 shows the 1980 proposed curriculum with Canadian information as the cornerstone of each grade; namely, Canadian human geography and world human geography, Canadian culture and world cultures, Canadian resource development and world resource development, Canadian governments and world government, and Canada's changing role in world concerns. It is basically a comparative approach. Column 3 summarizes a less radical change brought about subsequent to 1980 by teacher pressure for less dramatic change and insistence by the political level of the Ministry on British Columbian and Canadian content. The organizing focus of the grade 8 course, Canadian heritage, provides an appropriate framework for

Sequence of Content — British Columbia

1968 Draft Curriculum

Grade Seven: Culture Stages (Mediterranean Geography: History from earliest man to Feudal Ages)

Grade Eight: Developing Tropical World (Asia, Africa, Latin America, Renaissance, Evolution & Revolution) Renaissance, British or French Revolution)

Grade Nine: Industrial-Urban Regions Overseas (Japan, U.S.S.R., Europe) 19th Century and Contemporary World (Industrialization, Nationalism, W.W.I, W.W.II

Grade Ten: Canada in its North American Setting (Economic geography, Pacific, Continental Interior, Industrial Heartland) Canada in her North American Setting (Struggle for Continent to Macdonald Era, 1896)

Grade Eleven: Geography of World problems (Population, Urbanization) Canada in her World Setting (1896 — Present)

1980 Draft Curriculum

Grade VII: People and Places (Canada at present; Canada past: pre-contact and First European settlement; World present: Southern Temperate Climate (e.g. Aust.-N.Z.), World past: Mediterranean climate, 3000-1000 B.C.

Grade VIII: People and Cultures (World past: Greco-Roman to Reformation; Canada past: Immigration, 1604-1867; Canada present: B.C. or locale, Canada; World, present; U.S.A.

Grade IX: People and Resources (Canada, present; World past: Industrial Revolution; Britain, Canada past: development of B.C. and Western Canada, 1821-1914; World present: Mid-East, Far East)

Grade X: People and Government (Canada past: Confederation; Canada present: political and legal structures; World past: Russia to U.S.S.R., 1890-1930; World Present: Africa, developing nations)

Grade XI: People and the World (Canada's changing role in 20th Century; World concerns)

1984 Draft Curriculum

Grade 7: (Not included in 1984 redraft of secondary curriculum still titled People and Places).

Grade 8: Our Diverse Heritage (Geography plus Middle Ages in Western Europe, in Eastern Europe and Middle East, and in India, China, and Japan; Renaissance & Reformation in Europe; Exploration & Conquest; Current Developments).

Grade 9: No Title (North American geography, European settlements to 1815; Nation building: Europe, North America, & elsewhere; Industrialization in Europe & North America; Current Developments).

Grade 10: No Title (Confederation: causes & consequences; Development of West; Canada's resources & industries; Canada & the Pacific; Current Developments).

Grade 11: No Title (Government organization & power, emphasis on Canada; 20th Century & Canada; Global resources, geography & economic study, emphasizing 1st and 3rd worlds).

Topic C: Nationhood and Citizenship in Asia and Africa

GRADE EIGHT
PEOPLE AND THEIR INSTITUTIONS

In this topic, students examine an issue related to imperialism and the development of nations. One nation from each of the continents of Asia and Africa should be selected for comparison during the study.

Major attention should be given to four historical periods in the development of the nations studied: Pre-Imperialism, Western Domination, Struggle for Independence, Modernization since Independence.

Emphasis should be placed on how institutions have changed during these periods in the nations being studied. Inquiry should acknowledge the extreme difficulties that nations must contend with in attempting, at one and the same time, to be sensitive to an indigenous way of life while seeking aspects of modernization.

Competing Values and Social Issue
Modernization/Maintenance of Traditional Culture
Should developing nations strive to retain their indigenous culture and institutions or become part of the "modern" world?

VALUE OBJECTIVES	KNOWLEDGE OBJECTIVES	SKILL OBJECTIVES
Students will examine the social issue in order to develop the following understandings, competencies and attitudes. (Questions in italicized print are illustrative only.)	Students will gain understanding of the following generalization and concepts, as well as factual information appropriate to the inquiry questions that are listed.	Students will develop competence in the following inquiry and participation skills. Skills printed in standard type are emphasized for this topic.
1. Develop Understanding of Values	1. Generalization	1. Develop Inquiry Skills
1. Identify the values that are in conflict when developing nations attempt to respond to the basic needs of their citizens. — *What efforts have people in devel-*	Since gaining independence from colonial powers, less-developed nations have attempted to develop their economies while maintaining important cultural traditions.	1. Focus on the issue by identifying the conflict between the desire for modernization and desire to maintain cultural traditions. 2. *Establish research questions and*

procedures to investigate the issue in two nations across the four prescribed historical periods.

3. Gather and organize data by
   — reading original accounts (if available) which describe encounters between Westerners and Africans/Asians.
   — interpreting political maps of Africa/Asia before the imperialist powers arrived, just after W. W. II, and today.
   — reading bar and line graphs to interpret trends in population growth and economic development in Africa/Asia.
4. Analyze and evaluate data by comparing processes of modernization across the nations under study, checking for bias and the accuracy of documentation.
5. Synthesize data by formulating generalizations about the impact of imperialism on African/Asian nations, and problems of development experienced in these nations recently.
6. *Resolve the issue by examining the values underlying alternative strate-*

2. Concepts

1. Imperialism
2. Independence
3. Indigenous way of life
4. Economic development
5. International assistance

3. Questions to Guide Inquiry

1. What were some of the dominant features of the indigenous cultures of the societies selected for study?
2. Why did Western nations take over large parts of the world between 1870 and 1920? How did they justify their involvement in Asia and Africa?
3. What impact did imperialism have on institutions and culture in these countries?
4. What forces led to independence? What roles did key individuals play in struggles for independence?
5. What efforts to modernize have been made by these nations?
6. What aspects of their indigenous institutions and culture have they tried to retain?
7. What is the range of reactions among developing countries when Western nations offer economic assistance.

oping nations made to improve their standard of living? In what ways have they protected their culture and institutions from change? What values are demonstrated by these actions?

2. Develop Competencies

1. In value analysis, by identifying alternate solutions to the issue.
   — *Using the Role Exchange Test, what would be your present recommendation for resolution of the issue?*

3. Develop Attitudes

1. Of respect for the efforts of people in developing nations to resolve issues of cultural and institutional change.
2. Of open-mindedness, by being willing to view issues of modernization from the perspective of someone in a developing nation.
   — *Applying the Role Exchange Test, how do you think an individual in the country under study would view (specific instances of modernization in Canada?*

gies for improving the economy in African/Asian societies.

7. *Apply the decision by creating a for assisting developing nations through Canadian institutions.*

8. *Evaluate the decision by assessing the extent to which the above plan would strengthen indigenous institutions and also promote economic growth in a developing nation.*

2. Develop Participation Skills

1. Communicate effectively by writing a multiple paragraph composition to express and justify an opinion about developing nations.

2. *Interpret ideas and feelings of people in developing nations by by seeking to avoid stereotypes, and checking one's perceptions with other students.*

3. Participate in group work and decision-making by negotiating the allocation of tasks with group members.

4. *Contribute to a "sense of community" by helping create a plan of action to research the topic and resolve the issue.*

discussing our pluralistic roots in other cultures in an historical context. If the grade 9 course follows suit with an organizing title such as "Foundations of Nationhood," then it too will have Canadian relevance. The focus of the grade 10 course is clearly on Canada and, while weaker in grade 11, opportunities are available for a Canadian base. Perhaps what is most significant about this two-phase revision is that the Canadian orientation survived the compromise which the 1984 document represents.

An Evaluation

It is too early to assess the success of the British Columbia curriculum revisions. On the one hand, the greater Canadian emphasis ought to be quite successful, especially given its re-trial by a jury consisting of some thirty-nine B.C. educators, the vast majority of whom are teachers. However, there may still be some resentment to such a fundamental change instigated by the ministry, just as there may be a considerable reluctance to change focus on the part of some teachers. However, the compromise document of 1984 bodes well for the long-term maintenance of a Canadian orientation. A further sign of a serious commitment to this change is that the province has seen fit to consider proposals for the development of new materials, rather than choosing from those already published.

It is similarly too early to assess the Alberta effort. The teachers are demanding retraining and orientation sessions to help them teach the new curriculum. The reaction of individual teachers and students has been mixed. With regard to the teaching materials of the Heritage Project, a close reading of a formal ministry-initiated evaluation indicates that much refining needs to be done in terms of packaging and presentation so that the content will get maximum exposure to the targetted audience.

Notwithstanding Alberta's problems in undertaking such a massive project, the curriculum revisions and the material produced are transforming and Canadianizing the social studies curriculum throughout all grades. To some extent, the same idea on a much smaller scale is being repeated in other provinces in Canada, especially in the Atlantic region. Each of the four Atlantic provinces has commissioned or is commissioning provincial (and regional) histories for use either in the later elementary or the junior high grades. These initiatives are important for two reasons. First, there are the histories themselves. Second, and perhaps more importantly, is the recognition of responsibility by provincial education ministries for regional and national content.

Junior High Learning Materials

Teaching social studies at the junior high and, indeed, at the senior high level has been beset by a succession of problems. In historical review, having won the battle to get Canadian history and geography included in the curriculum, the problem became the type of history taught. (Geography did not and does not seem to be so much of a problem.) As Hodgetts[14] found in 1968, the history taught in Canadian schools as evidenced in both textbooks and classroom practice was a bland, constitutional history. It was often taught with a limited number of resources, all of which offered a single vision of our country's development. It failed to stimulate the involvement of the students because it failed to make history live.

From a different perspective than that of Hodgetts, Close and Bartels have pointed to the unconsidered, regime-supportive vision which runs through the vast majority of history textbooks. As they state it:

> In North America, regime-supportive approaches to political and socio-economic phenomena (a) support or condone the foreign policy of the Canadian and American governments; and (b) either tacitly or explicitly assert the superiority of the political and economic systems in Canada, the United States, and other liberal democracies over other political and economic systems.[15]

In one paragraph Close and Bartels list fifteen topics which receive a regime-supportive approach. They are: the Allied invasion of the Soviet Union (1917-1922); the rise of fascism; World War II; the Truman doctrine; the Marshall Plan; the Berlin Blockade; the Korean War; the IndoChina War; the Chinese Revolution; Soviet agriculture; the socialist countries of Eastern Europe; the coup in Iran which brought the Shah to power; the white regime of South Africa; Third World underdevelopment; and the Yalta Conference. In their reference section they list alternative interpretations for each topic.[16]

A third problem has been and is the major differences between anglophone and Quebec-based francophone perspectives on the history of Canada. In a study done in the late 1960s for the Bilingual and Bicultural Commission,[17] Trudel and Jain recommended development of materials incorporating both perspectives, a recommendation which has not been received enthusiastically in the light of provincial and school board purchases of a textbook developed by Trudel and others to meet that need.[18]

A last problem with history books is the presence of American-derived interpretations and American history where Canadian facts and interpretations should be. In looking at the materials used in Manitoba in the mid-1970s, Matchan found that in *Canada — A New Land,*[19] by Edith Deyell and published by Gage, there were 70 pages of American history in 496 pages. In one chapter called "England on the Atlantic Coast," Newfoundland is dismissed with expedition — "The French agreed to leave Placentia Bay and gave up their claim to Newfoundland forever." But life in Virginia and the other thirteen colonies is discussed in depth. Quebec's failure to join the thirteen colonies in 1775 is portrayed as stubbornness. Matchan also has noted the following:

Other curious features of the textbook include a pictorial essay of the Boston Tea Party, a section on the provisions of the American Constitution, a chapter on Texas and Oregon joining the Union, a biography of George Washington, a full-page description, complete with an illustration, of New York City, and a five-page excerpt from the diary of Benjamin Franklin.[20]

The book's sequel, *Canada — A New Nation*,[21] is no better by her account. The hero of the book is Lincoln. Two chapters are devoted to his life. Sir John A. Macdonald is portrayed as a man who "drank heavily and . . . did not behave as people might have hoped a Prime Minister would behave." One chapter is entitled "America sets a Pattern for Canadian Business."

Matchan also looked at two other textbooks, *Fair Domain*,[22] by George Tait, published by McGraw-Hill Ryerson, and *Canada in North America to 1800*,[23] by George Brown, Eleanor Harman, and Marsh Jeanneret, published by Copp Clark. There, amidst a plethora of American pictures, she found few "diagrams, pictures or descriptions of Canadian heroes, clothing, furniture or homes."[24] Brown et al. clearly articulate a colonial mentality by invidious comparison of the Upper Canada rebellion of 1837 to the British and American struggles of 1812.

In spite of the persistent major problems over the years, more satisfactory histories have begun to be published and to revive the longer standing eastern Canadian commitment to Canadian content. In 1977 two such histories seemed to start the trend, *In Search of Canada*[25] and *Forming a Nation*.[26] However, both fell prey to readability problems and a central Canadian bias. The result was that the Atlantic region tended to be forgotten as history progressed while the west was discussed largely within the context of the needs of central Canada. More recent histories for the grade 7 or 8 level have succeeded in being accepted through a combination of a greater regional sensitivity with a below-grade readability. Some examples are Macmillan's *Canada: Immigrants and Settlers* (1979),[27] Fitzhenry and Whiteside's *Growth of a Nation* (1980),[28] Globe/Modern's *Canada: A Growing Concern* (1981),[29] and Prentice-Hall's *Discovering Canada* (1982).[30]

Social Studies in Senior High

Because textbooks proceed almost chapter-by-chapter through what is outlined in provincial curriculum guidelines at the senior high level, we will discuss both textbooks and the curriculum in one section.

The curriculum revisions of Alberta and British Columbia demonstrate, at least to some degree, a basic Canadian orientation. British Columbia falls short with the exclusion of Canada in grade 12, the Alberta curriculum inadequately discusses Canada's global responsibilities in grades 11 and 12. Although resources are a central topic in Alberta, an analysis of

Canada's position in the world with regard to resources, and indeed the internal problems of resource division and distribution amongst the provinces, is not presented. An outdated bilateral, capitalist versus communist, world view is implicit in the grade 12 course. British Columbia does a better job in conceptualizing its curriculum, at least for grades 10 and 11.

In all other provinces, except Saskatchewan, Manitoba, and Ontario, a student can take Canadian history, social studies, or geography in at least two senior grades. Such a choice is only available at one level in the senior grades for those other three provinces. Despite that, a certain amount of Canadian content is contained in other courses in those provinces such as North American geography.

The real problem in assessing the adequacy of the senior level curriculum is that few provinces require students to complete a full sequence of social studies courses to graduate, and many provinces allow students to select from various social science and other socially oriented courses such as religion and law. These courses are optional substitutes for social studies, geography, and history. In the most extreme case, Alberta introduces studies in eleven different areas: social studies, history, geography, political science, anthropology, economics, sociology, religious studies, psychology, philosophy, and law.

One might expect little Canadian content in many of these courses. That is the case. In philosophy, psychology, and religious studies, for example, there is no provision for Canadian considerations in the approach taken to the subject. In political science, sociology, anthropology, and economics, the course outlines indicate that Canadian content may be used as an example, but the course is not structured to make it mandatory nor is it encouraged. For instance, sociology is divided into three units: "Culture and Society," "Institutions, Minorities and Social Behaviour," and "Applications of Sociological Concepts." Although there is room for a profoundly Canadian orientation here, Canadian content is peripheral in the minds of the course designers. In the listed reference material, two American texts are listed as "Primary References." Following that, seemingly as an afterthought, is a heading "Canadian content." Under this heading are listed three more limited Canadian works.[31]

Obviously the significance of the introduction of numerous options for the issues addressed here depends upon actual enrolments. There, the story is mixed and apt to change quickly as specific provincial regulations change. Table 2.2 outlines the picture of enrolments in the social sciences and philosophy in three provinces. While there are considerable differences between the provinces, the general level of enrolments in non-Canadian-oriented options is certainly sufficient to warrant concern for the extent to which high school students graduate with a sufficient knowledge of their own country.

The introduction of the social *sciences* at this level leads to another set of problems. The social sciences are introduced by emphasizing the power and structure of the discipline thereby capitalizing on what Piaget has iden-

Table 2.2 / Enrolments in Senior High Social Science and Philosophy

Subject	Province		
	Alberta[1]	Saskatchewan[2]	Nova Scotia[3]
Total Eligible Students (approx.)	36 000	15 000	13 000
Economics	1098	5572-9734	5578
Law	1994-8645*	1289-1910	4888
Sociology	1	1812	1397
Politics	13	22-160	647
Psychology	6461	1279-1700	
Anthropology	589		
Philosophy	182		

1. Alberta Education, Government Documents: unclassified.
2. Saskatchewan, Government Documents: unclassified.
3. Nova Scotia, Government Documents: unclassified.

tified as the major (mental) preoccupations of adolescents: hypothesizing, theorizing, and thinking in the abstract. The social science disciplines promote a vision of the relationship between the individual and society as that of the disinterested inquirer. This is quite opposite to exploring the role of the individual in helping to develop, maintain, and enhance a culture, surely the role of every member of a culture and the appropriate focus of the school system. Emphasis upon a disinterested or "objective" view tends to deny the very elements which are basic to the concrete, Canadian-based perspective we are arguing for throughout this book. It takes a sensitive social science indeed to build purposefully upon the culture from which it emanates. That brand of social science has yet to emerge in Canada.

The other major recent change which has been introduced at the senior high level is based on the influx of new materials, especially for the grades 9 and 10 level. Educational publishers have not been deaf to the cry for more Canadian materials over the past five to ten years. As a result, many newly published interdisciplinary Canadian studies materials are on the market. Unfortunately, the approach of such materials as *Canada's Century*,[32] *Canada Today*,[33] *Canadian Studies: Self and Society*,[34] and *Spotlight Canada*[35] is one which repeats the major problem with the type of history written for junior high. Without exception these books deal with issues of central importance or concern to the dominant cultural group. Only francophones receive attention as a "multicultural" group, and then

---

*Two numbers indicate enrolment extremes in courses which are taught over two or three grades.

only as the major cultural concern of the dominant group. An historian, Paul Bennett, has also severely criticized these books as lacking in the depth of understanding which can be acquired by utilizing the very sound research which Canadian historians have undertaken and published in recent years.[36]

Material being published for courses on multiculturalism and the design of the curriculum for minority groups present a vivid contrast. Multicultural materials such as Academic Press' *Origins*[37] deal with social realities not touched upon in the mainstream social studies books. Likewise the "multiculturalism" curriculum is sometimes especially adapted so that minority groups in the provinces are introduced to their own history. However, such courses are not intended for the dominant mainstream group; they read of and are taught about a unicultural world.

Summary and Conclusions

As this chapter points out, Canadian cultural content in social studies programs has recently become much more central to the curriculum than it has been in the past. We no longer need to identify the presence or absence of Canadian content, especially in the elementary and junior high grades, because if it is not there, it is in the process of being included within the curriculum. Henceforth we must analyse the appropriateness of the perspective on Canada and Canadians found in the curriculum and in learning materials.

There are still shortcomings in various provinces, at various levels, and with a number of materials. At the elementary level the first priority needs to be the development of regionally sensitive, nationally based materials reflective of our cultural roots which are also designed so that teachers can use them to their full potential. Clearly this task cannot be undertaken solely by a concentration of effort on the design of the curriculum and learning materials. It will also require a major commitment to teacher education directly focussed on this task.

At the junior high level the first task must be to ensure that the Canadian material entering the curriculum is both appealing to students and not superficial. Provincial curriculum departments and publishers would do well to keep abreast of contemporary writings in Canadian history, especially Canadian social history. All signs point to a rich vein of material which could readily be mined for the junior high school.

At the senior high level the major problem is to define the appropriate role for Canadian information and analysis in the final grades. The current situation betrays the efforts of the earlier grades in that, having written in a firm Canadian foundation up to the senior grades, the development of sophisticated analytical and cognitive skills in a Canadian context is now discarded in favor of encouraging such skills in a global context. The provision of social science options, the use of packaged materials dealing with Western civilization which contain no reference to Canada, the lack of a bold discussion of contemporary internal and world issues, can all be seen as equivalent to a betrayal. They betray the principle that a thorough study of one's own community, nation, and civilization carried through to the highest level of maturity is the firmest foundation for an understanding, a curiosity, and an appreciation of the world community.

However, there are signs of improvement. Curricula are being redefined, materials development is opening up for greater participation by Canadian publishers, and teachers are attempting to find a firmer Canadian footing for their teaching. Perhaps one might best summarize the situation by saying that a positive cultural perspective is returning to social studies. That cultural perspective is centred upon a desire for Canadian school children to learn about their country and its place in the world, to understand its identity and the values of its people in terms of its history and current priorities. Such changes hold a great deal of promise even if, as yet, they remain tenuous.

Footnotes

1. G. Redden, "Social Studies: A Survey of Provincial Curricula at the Elementary and Secondary Levels (Council of Ministers of Education of Canada, 1977).
2. B. Vass et al., *Social and Environmental Studies* (Toronto: McGraw-Hill, 1974).
3. G. H. Bevan, "Learning Resources: A Bookworm's Eye View of the Future," in G. H. Bevan, ed., *1980 Publishers' Conference*, Calgary, June 23-24, 1980 (Edmonton: Department of Education).
4. J. Fraser, "The Circular 14 Story: Approved Textbooks in Ontario," *Orbit*, 10(4), 8-9.
5. G. Scott, *English E1-Hi Publishing in Canada, 1980-1986* (Toronto: Pepper Wood, 1980).
6. D. Birch, R. Neering, and S. Garrod, eds., *One World: Primary and Intermediate Social Studies Picture Set* (Toronto: Fitzhenry & Whiteside, 1972).
7. D. Birch, personal communication.
8. B. Griffiths and E. A. Griffiths, *Canada: Our Roots and Environment* (Toronto: Gage, 1980).
9. Alberta, Department of Education, *Experiences in Decision-Making* (Edmonton: Department of Education, 1972).
10. L. Downey, *The Social Studies in Alberta: A Summary of a Report of an Assessment* (Edmonton: Alberta Education, 1975).
11. Manitoba, Department of Education, Submission to Council of Ministers of Education, Canada, for social studies curriculum survey.
12. Alberta, Social Studies Curriculum Committee, *1981 Alberta Social Studies Curriculum* (Edmonton: Alberta Education, 1981).
13. British Columbia, Ministry of Education, *Proposed Curriculum Guide, Social Studies K-11*, Draft Only, April 1980.
14. A. B. Hodgetts, *What Culture? What Heritage?* (Toronto: Ontario Institute for Studies in Education, 1968).

15. D. Close and D. Bartels, "The Socializing Effect of Regime Supportive Textbooks: First Results and Second Thoughts", *Socialist Studies* 1, 1979, p. 85.
16. Close and Bartels, "The Socializing Effect of Textbooks," p. 88.
17. M. Trudel and G. Jain, *Canadian History Textbooks: A Comparative Study* (Ottawa: Royal Commission on Bilingualism and Biculturalism, 1970).
18. The textbook in question is *Canada: Unity in Diversity* by P. G. Cornell, J. Hamelin, F. Ouellet, and M. Trudel (Toronto: Holt, Rinehart and Winston, 1967).
19. E. Deyell, *Canada: A New Land* (Toronto: Gage, 1970).
20. L. Matchan, "This is Supposed to be Canadian History," *Winnipeg Tribune,* 4 October 1975, p. 10.
21. E. Deyell, *Canada: A New Nation* (Toronto: Gage, 1970).
22. G. Tait, *Fair Domain* (Toronto: McGraw-Hill Ryerson, 1960).
23. G. Brown, E. Harman, and M. Jeanneret, *Canada in North America to 1800* (Toronto: Copp Clark, 1950).
24. Matchan, "This is Supposed to be Canadian History," p. 11.
25. R. Kirbyson and E. Peterson, *In Search of Canada: I* (Toronto: Prentice-Hall, 1977).
26. R. Stewart and N. McLean, *Forming a Nation: The Story of Canada and Canadians* (Toronto: Gage, 1977-78).
27. I. Hundley, *Canada: Immigrants and Settlers* (Toronto: Gage, 1979).
28. S. Garrod, *Growth of a Nation* (Toronto: Fitzhenry & Whiteside, 1980).
29. A. D. Hux and F. Jarman, *Canada: A Growing Concern* (Toronto: Globe/Modern, 1981).
30. R. Kirbystone, *Discovering Canada: Settling a Land* (Toronto: Prentice-Hall, 1982).
31. Alberta Education, Curriculum Outline, *Sociology.*
32. A. S. Evans and I. L. Martinello, *Canada's Century* (Toronto: McGraw-Hill Ryerson, 1978).
33. D. J. McDevitt et al., *Canada Today* (Toronto: Prentice-Hall, 1979).
34. I. Monro et al., *Canadian Studies: Self and Society* (Toronto: Wiley, 1975).
35. J. Cruxton and W. Wilson, *Spotlight Canada* (Toronto: Oxford, 1980).
36. P. V. Bennett, *Rediscovering Canadian History: A Teacher's Guide for the '80s* (Toronto: Ontario Institute for Studies in Education, 1980).
37. J. Saint and J. Reid, *Origins: Canada's Multicultural Heritage* (Toronto: Academic Press, 1979).

3: Canadian Educators: The Captured Profession

Introduction

The curriculum is created and implemented by particular groups of people, including teachers, professors, curriculum advisors, curriculum development officers and directors, other educational administrators and bureaucrats, and finally politicians. The common element amongst all but the politicians, and sometimes it includes them, is professional educational training. This chapter examines teacher training and teacher trainers. Firstly, we will review the teacher training curriculum, specifically including the content of teaching subjects (what the teacher teaches in the classroom) and foundation courses (which provide the teacher with a background understanding and philosophy of education). Secondly, we will outline the social and academic backgrounds of education professors to describe what they bring, as a group, to the task of training teachers. Thirdly, we will discuss the professional activities of professors as a further indication of their orientation to education. Finally, we will report upon a Statistics Canada survey to see what light it sheds on the backgrounds of education professors.

Canadian Programs of Teacher Certification

Student teachers take three types of courses. Because the methods course is of only marginal interest to this exploration, we will focus on the other two types of courses: teaching subject courses and foundation courses. The first type includes history, literature, mathematics, reading, physics and, more recently, such social sciences as anthropology, general psychology, and political science. They are advanced courses which give a deeper understanding of the subject area to future teachers. The second type of course includes sociology, anthropology, educational administration, legal foundations of education, history of education, educational and developmental psychology, and philosophy of education. These courses give teachers a general understanding of the educational process.

The content and relative number of courses in both these categories, together with the formal requirements or programs, constitute the operating philosophy of any teacher training program. In turn, these operating philosophies shape, to the extent that anything beyond the teachers' own schooling does, the outlook and attitudes of the Canadian teaching and education profession.

Requirements in Canadian Teacher Training

Table 3.1 shows the data collected on programs of faculties of education for at least one major institution in each province in Canada. In normal circumstances, a student teacher takes a maximum of 5 and a minimum of 3 full courses per year for a total program of anywhere between 16 and 25 full courses to complete the program. These figures are given as an anchor point for assessing the significance of the Canadian content requirements.

The data in Table 3.1 show that Canadian content is plainly not a priority in teacher training in the major Canadian institutions surveyed. No university in the survey requires more than one full course with Canadian content in the foundations. And only five of twelve universities have that minimal requirement. Also, no university requires any course with Canadian content in the teaching subjects.

The overall effect of this absence of Canadian requirements is that teachers lack the formal background to enable them to provide a Canadian foundation for classroom learning. They are ill-equipped to discuss Canadian examples which arise and to introduce Canadian examples when their textbooks fall short. For example, in a selection dealing with glaciers in *Reading 360*, the teacher's guide suggests students be asked to plot the cities near the border of the furthest glacial advancement during the last ice age.[1] As the majority of the cities lie in the United States, the exercise in reading comprehension becomes a lesson in American geography. A teacher with a background in Canadian geography could easily come up with an equally interesting exercise oriented to Canada. But Canadian geography is not required training for teachers who will teach Canadian geography, let alone for language arts teachers.

In a second example from a secondary history textbook, internal Canadian developments are compared unfavorably to events between Canada's historical masters. In *Canada in North America since 1800*, by Brown, Harman, and Jeanneret, the 1837 rebellion in Upper Canada is described as follows:

> When we think of some of the battles between the Americans and the British just twenty-five years earlier, the fighting that took place between the government troops and Mackenzie's rebels on December 7, 1837 seems very unimportant.[2]

Table 3.1/Required Canadian Content Courses in Selected Faculties of Education

University	Teaching Subjects	Foundations Courses
British Columbia	none	none
Simon Fraser	none	none
Alberta	none	Elementary: two courses in Canadian Studies and Social History of Canadian Education. Secondary: Intro to Canadian Education.
Calgary	none	none
Saskatchewan	none	Origins of Public Education.
Manitoba	none	one course Social Foundations (Canadian orientation).
Toronto	none	one full course, School Law in Ontario.
Ontario Institute for Studies in Education	not applicable	not applicable
McGill	none	none
New Brunswick	none	none
Dalhousie	none	none
Prince Edward Island	none	two half courses, Principles and Practices Canadian content.
Memorial	none	none

Why should the War of 1812 be considered more significant than the rebellion of 1837? More importantly, how could a teacher lacking a thorough grounding in Canadian history initiate a discussion of the comparative importance of the two events?

In *What Culture? What Heritage?*, Hodgetts provides examples of classroom practice in 1968 developed by teachers trained in programs similar to those that exist today. He found that faced with the task of teaching Canadian history, without a general background sufficient to allow them to take a fairly imaginative approach, teachers use essentially one of two methods: fact memorization or discussion. As Hodgetts points out, mere memorization of facts is not helpful to anyone, but the examples he cites indicate that when teachers lack sufficient background to be able to discuss Canadian material with any conviction, discussion can be even more dangerous.

> We observed . . . Canadian history classes . . . consciously designed to be "exciting, experimental and creative", which actually were occupied in aimless, undocumented chit-chat. This kind of "escape from Canadian history", one that seems to be growing in popularity, develops from the mistaken belief that "it does not matter what you teach, all that really counts is good discussion."[3]

Later he documents that "good discussion":

> "I think Confederation is a good thing."
> "I think it is a bad thing. I'm against it."
> "I'm for it."
> "What good will it do you?"
> "What harm will it do you?"
> "No harm, I just don't like it."
> "Well, I do."
> "Let's have a vote."[4]

Again in a discussion of Sir John A. Macdonald:

> "I say he was a drunkard."
> "Come off it, John, he liked his drinks but he wasn't a soak."
> "He got drunk right in public meetings."
> "Yeah, a real old wino."
> "I'll bet he didn't drink wine. I'll bet it was good Scotch."
> "Hah, just like my old man."[5]

The Downey Report portrayed social studies teaching as essentially the same in 1975.[6] And there is no reason to believe things are much different today in 1984.

In general, with regard to teaching subjects, teachers are not provided with a Canadian contextual background sufficient for them to understand how their subject matter contributes to the overall understanding we have of our nation. Instead they are introduced to their teaching subject as a discipline or process of inquiry. It appears that the teacher with a European, American, or Asian history or geography background is considered equally as capable of teaching Canadian history as is a teacher with a background in Canadian history or geography. Because of the prevalence of this attitude towards the content of a discipline, teachers come to see basic factual information as unimportant. They emphasize a "conceptual understanding" of the subject, which, as we have seen, students are capable of quickly reducing to a conceptual understanding of the parameters of the sobriety of our first Prime Minister, not something which gains anyone very much.

The situation regarding Canadian orientation in foundations courses is not quite as bleak as it is in teaching subjects. But that is like saying that an Arctic whiteout is not quite as bleak as one in the Antarctic. According to Table 3.1, five of the twelve universities surveyed have minimal Canadian-oriented requirements. The Universities of Alberta, Manitoba, Saskatchewan, and Prince Edward Island require courses which introduce current issues in Canadian education or Canadian education in an historical context. The University of Toronto has one compulsory course on the structural and legal base of education in Ontario. The other seven universities surveyed require no foundation courses with Canadian content.

Lacking courses in Canadian foundations, teachers are not given the background knowledge to talk with parents or each other about the general, national, social, or cultural context of education. They have little basis for requesting certain types of provincial, regional, or even national issues be included in the curriculum. They lack a broader exposure to what education is all about in Canada. What can they say about federal versus provincial involvement? About the overall content of the curriculum? About a national core curriculum? About the desirability of involving Canadian publishers? About the relation of educational programs and job requirements? Indeed, about the social and cultural context of education in Canada?

They can do little except fall back on their opinions as citizens or pursue advanced training. In doing the former they may fall prey to the standard bias of their particular ethnic group or region. For instance, many English Canadian teachers might think the federal government is more "sophisticated" than provincial governments and therefore should be more heavily involved in education. In doing the latter they find themselves leaving the classroom and entering administration or teaching teachers. Without courses introducing education within a Canadian social context, educators lack the sophistication to participate in what surely should be an active debate amongst all in the profession, that is, the framing of educational policy.

Canadian Content in Program Design

Examining explicit Canadian content in the formal descriptions of the requirements of teacher trianing programs is, admittedly, a rather limited perspective on the Canadian content question. A less limited approach is to examine educational foundation courses for the societal and cultural context they bring to their exploration of education. The presence of such a context indicates the degree to which they emphasize a perspective in which Canadian information might be considered as important.

Each of the areas of inquiry represented in the foundations provides a slightly different perspective on human affairs. For instance, anthropology emphasizes the cultural, sociology the social, psychology the individual, history the historical and comparative, philosophy the conceptualization of the entire enterprise. To provide a bit more detail, an educational psychologist examines children as "performing" units, isolating them from their environment as a whole. He or she then supplies the teacher with hints on how that performance can be improved. A sociologist tends to examine the structure of social interaction in the educational environment and relate it to some grand theory of society. An historian commonly relates the educational environment to certain viewpoints which have shown themselves to be vibrant in society. A philosopher attempts to provide an unambiguous analysis of exactly what is going on.

On the basis of their perspectives, the foundation courses can be divided into two categories. On the one hand, there is psychology and philosophy, neither of which introduce a context in which any discussion of cultural or national issues is entertained. On the other hand, the remaining foundations courses do introduce a cultural context, about 25 percent with Canadian specifics. The former courses can thus be referred to as "non-social" foundations; the latter as the "social" foundations. A comparison of the relative numbers of these two categories of courses provides a measure of the emphasis placed on a perspective where Canadian context might enter the discussion.

The most accurate picture of the balance between "social" and "non-social" foundations can be obtained by comparing the number of faculty hired to teach in each area. When that information is not available, the number of courses offered in each area can be compared. Tables 3.2 and 3.2a give the results of an analysis of faculty and courses which we undertook as part of this study. If not stated otherwise in the footnotes of the table, it should be assumed that the educational psychology category includes only those labelled educational psychology and that educational foundations includes sociology, anthropology, history, and philosophy.

In every university but Dalhousie, the data show that there are far more resources available to mount psychology courses than all other foundations courses together. Often there are twice as many psychology faculty and courses as there are faculty and resources to teach all the other foundations courses. Using this 2 to 1 ratio, if we look at the situation a little more closely by assuming that philosophy accounts for one-quarter of "educational foundations," and that 25 percent of the courses of other "social" disciplines have Canadian content — probably a generous assumption — the ratio of psychology to Canadian content is something in the order of *11 to 1*. Since it is rare for students to take eleven foundations courses, this means that the great majority of teachers graduate with foundations courses that have no Canadian content, an apparent parallel with the orientation of their expertise in the teaching subjects.

It is perhaps only slightly overstating the case to say that teachers are trained to function professionally completely out of the cultural context and, specifically, out of the Canadian context of their profession. Given the prevalence of psychology in the foundations, teachers cannot help but become oriented to children within the context of psychological or individual processes. In its simplest form, such a context promotes the idea

Table 3.2/Ratio of Numbers of Faculty Identified as Associated with Educational Psychology Compared to those Identified as Associated with Educational Foundations

University	Educational Psychology Professors/ Educational Foundations Professors
British Columbia[1]	73/31
Alberta	44/23
Calgary[2]	61/16
Saskatchewan	16/7
Manitoba	12/11
Toronto[3]	18/7
Ontario Institute for Studies in Education	29 + 40[4]/25
Memorial	14/10
Prince Edward Island[5]	--

1. Includes Counselling Psychology, Educational Psychology, and Special Education.
2. Includes Educational-Psychological Counselling and Clinical and School Counselling.
3. Includes Counselling, Institute of Child Study, and Special Education.
4. Includes 40 "Associated Faculty."
5. At the University of Prince Edward Island the five permanent faculty crossed disciplines. A meaningful ratio was not possible.

Table 3.2a*/Ratio of Numbers of Courses Offered in Educational Psychology Compared with the Number of Courses Offered in Educational Foundations

University	Educational Psychology Courses/ Educational Foundations Courses
Simon Fraser	10/7
McGill	41[6]/28[7]
New Brunswick	12/? (2 Canadian)[8]
Dalhousie	9/16

*In universities where faculty were not identified in a manner which differentiated their teaching responsibilities by their subject of expertise, the number of courses in educational psychology and educational foundations were calculated and placed in the form of a ratio.

Notes:
6. Foundations include Psychology and Sociology.
7. Includes Religion and Philosophy, Administration, and Politics.
8. Two Canadian courses identified by calendar descriptions.

that scholastic success depends on two things, one, the "intelligence" of the student, a questionable concept in itself, and two, the appropriateness of the teaching methods. Faced with success, the teacher feels that his or her students are intelligent and that his or her teaching methods are sound. Faced with failure, the teacher can call in the diagnostician to deal with his or her methods but more usually with the performance of the children. The *a priori* assumption of such a specialist is that whatever the problem, it is a matter of abnormal individual functioning. This assumption does not develop from observation, but purely because the remedial disciplines are psychology-derived.

Children's cultural backgrounds, of course, play a very large role in determining their scholastic success. Numerous studies indicate that lower performance levels amongst working-class populations in Canada are related not to differences in intelligence or individual motivation, but to the nature of the interaction between the education system and working-class culture. (See, for example, G. Martell, ed., *The Politics of the Canadian Public School.* Toronto: James Lorimer, 1974.) Yet the data and analyses of these studies are largely ignored by educators because they do not fit their working assumptions of education. The argument can be extended from the working class to all Canadians. The nature of the interaction between the education system and Canadian culture must allow Canadians to make maximal use of the experience and the knowledge they gain outside the school, as a basis for, and extension of, school learning. To do less not only makes learning needlessly difficult and distant from our lives, it is also culturally undermining.

The Role of School Boards

No formal Canadian content requirements to speak of, together with one chance in eleven of taking a Canadian-oriented foundations course, does not paint a rosy cultural picture of Canadian education. But perhaps school boards in the name of their communities demand an appropriate Canadian background in hiring teachers, especially for subjects like history. To address this issue we surveyed the hiring procedures of school boards across Canada to see what attention they paid to the Canadian orientation of those they hired. We asked several questions to get an overall picture of their attitude to Canadian content and a Canadian perspective. The questions were:

1. Is any preference in hiring given to teachers who have a knowledge of specific, Canadian subject matter over knowledge in a particular discipline? That is to say, would a potential teacher be preferred if his/her background had an emphasis on Canadian literature or history over a general specialty in literature or history?

2. Are teachers, once they are hired, encouraged (by the board or perhaps individual principals) to take in-service courses which have Canadian content?

3. Is any preference given to hiring Canadian citizens? (Non-Canadian citizens? Landed immigrants?)

4. Finally, does the board encourage teachers who are recent immigrants to take courses which might orient them to Canada?

Sixty-nine replies were received from a sample of 85 requests randomly selected within categories, with categories chosen to reflect region, population density, both language groups, and Roman Catholic as well as non-Catholic school boards for information. The answers to the questions were as follows:

(1) 74 percent of the respondents said no preference was given to teachers with a specific knowledge in Canadian subject matter over general knowledge in a discipline.

(2) 54 percent of the respondents said teachers were not encouraged to take Canadian content in-service training; 33 percent of the respondents said that teachers were encouraged to do so.

(3) 80 percent answered "yes" to question 3. Since we received rather perfunctory answers without explanations, we took these "yes's" to mean landed immigrants and Canadian citizens were given preference.

(4) 75 percent of the respondents reported they provided no encouragement to recent immigrant teachers to take courses which might orient them to Canada.

According to the above replies, at least 70 percent of school boards have no concern with Canadian content in the training and qualifications of teachers. Since there was a certain amount of equivocation by the respondents on many of the questions, it would be safe to say only 15 percent of school boards have a clear concern for Canadian-oriented training. And even that concern does not extend beyond a preference. Categorical Canadian-oriented hiring requirements are non-existent.

The Canadian Orientation of Education Professors

Canadian content may not be part of the requirements in teacher training; and it may not play a major role in the course offerings and content of education faculties; but it may still be there. Perhaps the professors in faculties of education are so imbued with a Canadian perspective that it becomes an unstated foundation of their teaching. This might be the case if faculty members are, in the overwhelming majority, born, raised, and partially trained in Canada, or if the great majority of faculty members at least culminated their training in Canada.

The reason for believing that either, but especially both, of these conditions might provide an undercurrent of Canadian concern to teacher training and in turn schooling is that childhood and adolescent experience as well as professional training are two major areas which contribute to the point of view professors take in their teaching. Childhood and adolescent experience provides the basis for the set of assumptions a person builds up about the individual, the small group, the community, the society, the state, institutions, and so on; if you like, a set of values. These assumptions and values provide a basic orientation for the curriculum of the school, the role of the expert versus the generalist teacher, the educational role of the parent, the relation between the school and the local community, the organization of the classroom, and so forth.

The second major component of a professor's basic outlook is his or her professional training. Professional training is not acultural. Training reflects the priorities and the style of the culture within which it is designed both in what is selected for study and in how that study is conceptualized.

A Case in Point

In 1966, an American was hired by the Ontario Institute for Studies in Education (OISE) to teach in the Department of Applied Psychology. His training at Syracuse University was in developmental psychology. His then current interest was moral education, specifically Lawrence Kohlberg's formulations of the developmental sequence of moral judgments. This particular professor was energetic and attractive and he supervised a number of graduate students, including the author, many of whom produced theses on Kohlberg's theory. Partially as a result of his enthusiasm other professors at OISE took up a parallel interest in Kohlberg's work. The OISE group was just one of many. In other centres, Canadian academics returning to Canada and foreigners hired to teach in Canada brought Kohlberg's formulations with them from their graduate work in the United States and even in the United Kingdom.

The end result has been that nearly every Canadian teacher, every Canadian graduate student in education, and most psychology undergraduates, have had at least passing exposure to Kohlberg's ideas. Many elementary and secondary schools have programs founded on Kohlberg's concept of moral judgment making. Teachers of social studies often justify working from a value perspective through their knowledge of Kohlberg's theories.

The irony is that many who initially imported Kohlberg's ideas have subsequently reassessed them. Many, but by no means all, now see them as applications of a rather conservative attitude to the social world reflective of the formal political structure of the United States.[7] Some have called Kohlberg's theory into serious question as a cross-culturally valid sequence of judgment making. As I see it, Kohlberg's formulations are an expression of the individualism central to American culture. They represent an application of the values of literacy and technology to the realm of social affairs. They mask cultural differences. They have nothing whatsoever to say about how the individual affirms his or her membership in a cultural group, while maintaining his or her sense of self and a set of ideals.

In spite of these somewhat belated cultural assessments, Kohlberg's form-

Table 3.3/Geographical Location of Degrees Received by Education Professors in a Selection of Canadian Universities, 1981-82 (percentages)

	UBC	SFU	Calgary	Alta*	Man.	McGill	Dal.	Mem.	Average
First Degrees									
Canada	63	54	64	72	66	57	54	64	60
Within Prov.	35	22	36	42	40	43	25	47	35
Out of Prov.	28	32	28	30	26	14	29	17	25
U.S.A.	28	19	22	22	22	23	21	19	22
U.K.	18	24	11	6	8	14	25	14	15
Other	1	3	3	0	3	5	0	1	2
Final Degrees									
Canada	34	36	39	42	42	49	67	50	45
Within Prov.	16	11	25	33	18	33	13	3	17
Out of Prov.	18	25	14	9	24	16	54	47	28
U.S.A.	60	53	47	56	54	41	21	47	46
U.K.	5	11	13	2	3	6	13	4	8
Other	1	0	1	0	1	4	0	0	1

*1978-79 data.

ulations have been introduced uncritically in many Canadian schools. The limitations of the perspective are not given much attention.

A General Picture

Table 3.3 summarizes data gathered to indicate the approximate extent to which like ideas are being imported to Canada. The figure illustrates the social and professional backgrounds of professors of education in the same selection of Canadian universities as was used for the other data reported in this chapter.

It gives some cause to take heart. Sixty percent of professors received their first degree from a Canadian university compared to 22 percent at American universities.

But 46 percent of professors received their final degrees in the United States while only 45 percent obtained final degrees in Canada. The number of professors who received their first and final degrees from a university in the province in which they are now teaching is 35 percent and 17 percent respectively.[8]

The patterns of the qualifications of professors at Memorial and Dalhousie warrant some discussion. At Memorial, there is a very high percentage of first degrees from the Atlantic region (47 percent), many of them Memorial degrees, together with a very low percentage of final degrees from the region (3 percent). At the same time a fair number of faculty have out-of-region Canadian first degrees (17 percent) and a high number of out-of-region Canadian final degrees (47 percent). This pattern is probably an indication of a sensitivity to local conditions in combination with a broader Canadian perspective. However, counteracting that sensitivity is the presence of a group of professors with U.S. final degrees equal in number to those with out-of-region Canadian degrees (47 percent).

Dalhousie's pattern indicates something else again. The low number of regional first degrees (25 percent) combined with a very low number of final regional degrees (13 percent) and a high number of out-of-region Canadian final degrees (54 percent) could inciate a fairly strong national orientation that is not overshadowed by the presence of faculty with American final degrees (21 percent).

The possibility that these two patterns of faculty training might result from a full fledged cultural concern could not be overlooked. Consequently, we reviewed the content of course offerings at both universities.

Because the teaching-subject and methods courses at Dalhousie indicate nothing unusual in the way of Canadian content, we looked to courses in educational foundations. As expected, none of the psychology or philosophy courses contain Canadian content. In the other foundations of the four sociology courses, in terms of a national perspective, one deals with China, none with Canada. History (of education) is the only field in which there are Canadian-oriented courses. Three of the five courses introduced "new education," progressive education, and educational issues. Each course discusses these ideas in a Canadian context.

This information seemed doubly disappointing. Despite being the only university surveyed with more courses and faculty in the foundations than in educational psychology, and despite a healthy complement of Canadian-trained academics, Dalhousie squanders the structural capability of addressing education from within a Canadian context.

Memorial's situation is more heartening. Of the twenty-seven courses in the foundations, slightly under half (twelve) have a Canadian orientation. Many of the common foundations courses are paired with ones which address the same issues from a Canadian context. For instance, "School and Society" is paired with "The School and the Community." Likewise, "Educational Administration" is paired with "Comparative Educational Administration." Many courses that commonly do not discuss Canadian matters directly such as "Education and Culture" contain a Canadian context according to their calendar descriptions. Canadian elements (with particular emphasis on northern, Native, and isolated communities) appear to be so entrenched in the program that they spill over into methods, teaching-subject courses, and some of the psychology-based courses. Six methods courses deal with teaching strategies, administration, communication, and teaching practices in northern, Native, and isolated community settings. One course is listed in Native literature, while one of nine courses dealing with exceptional children adopts a Canadian cultural viewpoint.

The strengths of Memorial's program are that it provides an overall Canadian context in the foundations followed up by the specifics entailed in teaching in settings common to Newfoundland and Labrador. Like much of the activity in the university as a whole, the Faculty of Education appears to be tightly integrated with the needs of the province and its people.

But what is the significance of the aggregate, cross-Canada data? The number of first Canadian degrees suggests that basic Canadian values and attitudes may be present in the outlook of (at least) the majority of professors through their childhood experience. However, their graduate training, area specialties, and course offerings do not give much confidence that a Canadian spirit pervades Canadian teacher training.

Another significant pattern is the number of faculty who have final degrees from the province in which they are now teaching. If we combine such individuals with those who have obtained American final degrees, the aggregate percentage of final degrees is 65 percent. Let us assume that those who have a final degree from a Canadian university *outside* the province in which they now teach are the backbone of a *national interchange* of educators and are the core group to conduct a national debate on Canadian education. The ratio of those with such a national background to those who have either a local or U.S.-based training is more than 2 to 1. Given that the ratio of non-Canadian content courses in the foundations to those having Canadian content was, at best, 11 to 1, the likelihood of national issues emerging as the core or even a peripheral issue of the professional training of teachers is extremely small.

Canadian Content in the Professional Activities of Education Professors

In spite of the grim picture painted so far, one last important question can usefully be asked. Are issues dealing specifically with education in Canada addressed within Canadian faculties of education through conference attendance by professors and through the contributions of professors to Canadian journals? To try to answer that question, we asked a random sample of over two hundred professors of education from the universities across the country listed in Tables 3.2 and 3.2a about their recent publications and the recent conferences they had attended.

Disappointingly, only seventy-six replied. As a result of the less than one-third response rate, the representativeness of the data can be questioned. Nevertheless, they are presented here for what they reveal.

There are four categories of location in Figure 3.1. "Local," with respect to conferences, refers to the region within which a professor teaches, namely, the Prairies, the Atlantic, Ontario, Quebec, or British Columbia. When used in reference to publications, it means that the editorial office of a regionally oriented publication is in the region in which the professor teaches. Thus the category does not include nationally oriented journals such as *Interchange*. The categories "Canadian" and "American" are self-explanatory. "Other" includes Britain, eastern and western Europe, and Australia.

The data indicate that Canadian and local journals and conferences are not spurned by professors teaching in Canada. But professors also attend conferences and have articles published in the United States with nearly equal frequency to the amount they publish and attend conferences locally and nationally. In short, the United States is as strong a point of professional reference for both individuals and departments as is Canada and the region combined.

So the answer to the weakest possible question of whether a concern for Canadian realities through Canadian professional communication about education exists is a qualified and somewhat hesitant "yes."

Two Disturbing Examples

Given the state of teacher training and the study of education which has been outlined, it is useful to introduce some concrete examples of how a distinctive Canadian orientation and distinctive Canadian problems become swamped by a lack of separation between American, pan-national, and Canadian questions.

To cite a first example, not so long ago a British educational philosopher, Robin Barrow, came to the University of Western Ontario for one year. Barrow undertook to write a book while in Canada, entitled *The Canadian Curriculum: A Personal View,* now published by the University of Western Ontario Press. The book purports to be an exploration of the Canadian cur-

Figure 3.1/Geographical Location of the Three Most Recent Conferences Professors Attended and the Editorial Offices of the Three Journals in Which Professors Most Recently Published.

Sample distributions by university

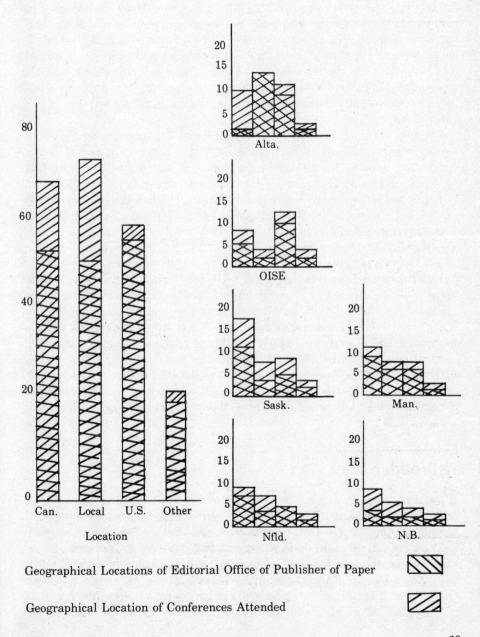

Geographical Locations of Editorial Office of Publisher of Paper

Geographical Location of Conferences Attended

riculum and classroom practice in an historical and contemporary context complete with commentary on teacher training. In fact, it consists of the impressionistic ramblings of a British philosopher ensconsed for a winter in London, Ontario. The "Canadian" curriculum is dealt with in the most cursory and peripheral way and only to be dismissed as trivial or misguided. For instance, one chapter, which deals with the contribution of "radicals" to educational thought, ends with one paragraph noting three Canadian references. It miscites one, and says nothing more than that Canadian radicals have addressed much the same issues as have the American radicals cited and discussed in the chapter. The pity is that, attracted by the promising title, and a major publicity campaign with monthly ads in *The Canadian Forum,* 3000 or more earnest buyers have purchased Barrow's book. Will Barrow be the last foreigner encouraged to undertake an instant analysis of the appropriateness of the national orientation of our curriculum?

A second example. Several years ago, an American who received his final degree in a Canadian institution set up a summer program at Simon Fraser University to bring six outstanding scholars to the campus. Of the first six scholars, one was a Canadian of British birth, one was a new Canadian of American birth, and the other four were Americans. At a public address one of the American "experts" suggested that Canada needed an educational system capable of producing cultural heroes such as Helen Keller, Theodore Roosevelt, or Abe Lincoln (his examples). He argued that Canada needed to create priorities in its educational thinking that were exactly parallel to what he advocated for the United States. We were to implement identical solutions to our assumed identical problems in order to achieve identical aims. When challenged on the grounds that his solution was characteristically American, in that he wished us to design a system to produce individuals personally capable of battling against misguided institutions, the chair of the session and the audience immediately rose to the defence of the American expert. Moreover, they did so in a way which made it apparent that they saw no cultural issue in the outsider's definition, analysis, and solution, even though it was steeped in American perspectives and lore.

A Broader View

Why is there such a ready acceptance of the analyses and solutions of others? In this chapter Canadian teacher training programs have been examined in some depth. That examination has shown there to be a prevailing non-Canadian and therefore non-cultural orientation to teacher training complementary to the attitudes which dominate curriculum development and which hold sway in educational publishing. However, although the picture which has been painted is accurate and representative, it is not complete. The contributory factors to the general outlook of the education profession are many and varied. It would be illustrative to mention several other influences in passing which consolidate the effects and attitudes which have been identified in the foregoing pages.

Representatives of a non-cultural and non-Canadian perspective surround teacher training and the profession. For instance, many education professors of such teaching subjects as mathematics or language arts invite publishers' reps to give lectures on their programs to student teachers. The purpose of such lectures is to give student teachers an overview of the materials they will probably be using once they start teaching. While such a practice is defended as "realistic," in fact it merely legitimates those publishers with an already strong position in the market, namely, the U.S.-based multinationals. When such professors neglect to teach a basic understanding of the subject matter and the principles upon which it might be taught, these new teachers graduate without the ability to do anything but choose between the various series produced by these multinationals.

Similar non-cultural influences can be found elsewhere in the education profession. One of the more formidable in Canadian education is a fraternity called Phi Delta Kappa. This American-based organization is the professional equivalent of the business multinational. That is to say, it is an American-based, international educational society with Canadian branch organizations which does not capture markets but captures the attention of professionals by creating channels of professional communication. A review of its journal, *Phi Delta Kappan,* shows that the questions addressed over the years are those at the forefront of American education. It is not that Canadians do not contribute to the journal, rather they contribute to a discussion of issues common to the education system of Canada, the U.S., and other countries as well. The final result is that a market for American ideas is developed, helped along by branch meetings of Canadian educators who bring in high-profile American speakers.

The activities and approach of Phi Delta Kappa are not unusual in the profession and should not be condemned as atypical. Only a few years ago the Canadian Teachers Federation (CTF) held a national conference entitled "The Quality of Education in Canada." The keynote speaker was an American, Neil Postman, author of several books on education, none of which deal specifically with Canada and the best known of which is *Teaching as a Subversive Activity.* Few would deny that Postman has some interesting insights, but there are certain equally capable Canadians who might address the same issues, especially within the framework of the conference as indicated in its title.

Again here, this conference and the CTF are not atypical. It is not difficult to come across numerous national and regional Canadian conferences where not a single Canadian is asked to speak. Moreover, faculties of education in the name of professionalism often ensure the continuance of such a bias. For example, universities often have professional programs approved by professional bodies. For instance, the reading program at the University of Alberta is approved by the American-based International

Reading Association (IRA). The structure and cultural orientation of this body is parallel to that of Phi Delta Kappa. The IRA is an international, American-based, professional body which sets the agenda for issues in the field. They are successful in their agenda-setting role not only because they are a point of focus within the profession, but also because they are effective lobbyists with private research foundations who support research and thus advance the careers of academics. As Canadian educational researchers choose their research questions, they must court the favor of these agencies, ones such as the Ford and Mott Foundations. These bodies have a number of priorities which they establish in consultation with their U.S.-based advisors. They are not at all unwilling to fund Canadian academics but to study problems the foundation sees as significant. The pity, of course, is that the chosen priorities rarely allow a consideration of the cultural issues of our discussion in this book.

Update

In December 1981, Statistics Canada released a study[9] done primarily as background for the recently published third volume of the Commission on Canadian Studies.[10]

The study, entitled "Foreign Academics at Canadian Universities: A Statistical Perspective on New Appointments during the Seventies," concentrates on a wide sampling of new appointments, legal status of faculty and their first degrees (note not final degrees!), and thus contrasts with the data presented here.

As background, the study points out that "in 1977-78, more than half [58 percent] of all full-time faculty had obtained their [first] degree in Canada." The high was in education at 70 percent and the low was in fine and applied arts at 45 percent. An examination of the trends over the years 1972-73 to 1980-81 for all subject areas shows a slight increase (5 percent) in the number of newly appointed faculty who obtained their first degrees from Canada. A greater and more regular increase (12 percent) was found in the number of newly appointed faculty who were Canadian citizens. While these two sets of figures, considered separately, might look like modest but encouraging gains, the latter especially, they also point to another rather disturbing trend when put together. A comparison of the two groups points out that a steadily *increasing* number of faculty (10 percent) took first degrees outside Canada over the nine-year period (see Table 3.4).

Several other interesting findings appear in Statistics Canada's data. Over the last four years of the study, 1977-81, 84 percent of new appointments were either Canadian citizens or long-standing permanent residents and 9 percent received their permanent resident status upon appointment. In the final three years of the study *in education*, 91 percent of appointments were given to Canadian citizens or long-term permanent residents. (Education ranked highest among the disciplines.)

Table 3.4/Percentage of Newly Appointed Full-Time University Faculty Holding Canadian Citizenship and Having Received Canadian First Degrees, 1972-73 to 1980-81

Year of Appointment	Canadian Citizens %	First Canadian Degree %	Percentage Difference
1972-73	59.1	55.7	3.4
1973-74	63.3	59.2	4.1
1974-75	62.4	57.4	5.0
1975-76	64.2	57.5	6.7
1976-77	65.3	57.2	8.1
1977-78	69.2	59.4	9.8
1978-79	73.7	64.3	9.4
1979-80	72.0	60.6	11.4
1980-81	71.6	60.8	10.8
Nine Year Total	66.9	58.9	8.0

Such figures give some reason to be optimistic. However, two points must be borne in mind. The first is that we have no data on final degrees. While the hiring of Canadians should be lauded, if the majority of Canadians continue to receive their graduate training in the U.S., the reculturation of Canadian education will be slow indeed. The second point, that the gains being made in citizenship are almost being equalled by a tendency of Canadians to take first degrees outside the country, gives reason for some considerable pessimism.*

---

*Inquiries made subsequent to the drafting of this chapter produced a limited amount of data on location of final degree of university faculty. The data indicated no dramatic divergence from the general picture presented here. They can be summarized in the following statements. As of 1979-80, 83 percent of all faculty teaching education in Canadian universities are Canadian citizens. The following table shows the countries from which these professors received their final degrees.

Faculty Citizenship	Country of Final Degree (Percentage)			
	Canada	U.S.	U.K.	Other
All Faculty	50	41	3	6
Canadians	57	36	3	4
Non-Canadians	15	69	7	9

Summary and Conclusions

The orientation of teacher training in Canadian faculties of education, at least in those sampled, is relatively clear. Teachers are not given a Canadian orientation either to their particular subject or to education in general. They are not given such an orientation because professors do not see it as basic to the task of training and educating teachers. Professors do not see a Canadian orientation as central, perhaps, because too many are American-raised or -trained; because school boards appear unconcerned; and because careers are most easily advanced through American-oriented professional activity. With the exception of Memorial, not enough faculty members come from, or are trained in, Canada and specifically in provinces other than the one in which they teach. However, two tentative trends provide some reason for a little optimism. First, an increasing number of Canadians are being hired to teach in Canadian universities. Given our economic downturn, it would be surprising to find anything but such a trend. Secondly, Canadian seminars, annual conferences, and publications indicate at least a minimal concern for Canadian matters exists, if only because of the individual self-interests of faculty members in their careers.

Footnotes

1. T. Clymer, ed., *Reading 360* (Toronto: Ginn Canada, 1972).
2. G. Brown, E. Harman, and M. Jeanneret, *The Story of Canada* (Toronto: Copp Clark, 1950).
3. Hodgetts, *What Culture? What Heritage?*, p. 28.
4. Hodgetts, *What Culture? What Heritage?*, p. 53.
5. Hodgetts, *What Culture? What Heritage?*, p. 68.
6. L. Downey, *The Social Studies in Alberta: A Summary of a Report of an Assessment* (Edmonton: Alberta Education, 1975).
7. E. V. Sullivan, personal communication.
8. In the cases of the Atlantic provinces, because of their size, the small number of graduate education programs and the distinctiveness of the region as a whole, "within the province" has been interpreted to mean "within the Atlantic provinces."
9. M. von Zur Muehlen, "Foreign Academics at Canadian Universities: A Statistical Perspective on New Appointments during the Seventies," mimeo paper, December 1981.
10. T. H. B. Symons and J. E. Page, *Some Questions of Balance: Higher Resources, Higher Education and Canadian Studies* (Ottawa: Association of Universities and Colleges of Canada, 1984).

4: The Creation and Selection of Learning Materials

In outlining the training of teachers in the previous chapter, we identified patterns which orient educators to perceive education in an acultural or non-Canadian context. In this chapter, we shall exmaine the influence which the selection and adoption of learning materials has on the Canadian orientation of education.

The Workings of the Marketplace: What Control Do Educators Have over Learning Materials?

On the surface of it, learning materials enter Canadian classrooms in the following manner:

1. Curriculum committees, most often composed of teachers, provincial department of education personnel, and professors, review the present curriculum and write a new curriculum outline.

2. Once the new curriculum is approved by the department, submissions are formally called for from publishers and are reviewed both by the curriculum committee and by hired experts.

3. Depending upon the province, either one set or a variety of materials are selected and approved for use within the province.

However, the detailed story is much more interesting, intricate, and intriguing.

A Preliminary Perspective

It would be easy to claim educators dominate the scene in the creation, selection, and adoption of learning materials because most educational texts are written by educators, reviewed by educators, and selected for use at all levels in the educational hierarchy by educators. But while educators participate at every level, so do publishers.

Publishers select authors and editors to develop ideas, often those of the publisher. Publishers bring research and opinion into the public domain which then provide the context for other practical publications such as school texts. Publishers look at the material needs of educators then suggest how their products meet that need. Publishers continually update their intimate knowledge of curriculum development procedures and curriculum content. Publishers reward the bright and energetic with publication which, in turn, gives them power and influence in the selection of materials for use in schools.

The long and short of it is that the large traditional educational publishers turn up everywhere in the educational system. Their omnipresence not only creates enormous influence, but also leads to confluences and conflicts of interest. Conflicts of interest arise from professors who have published a book, for example, in curriculum theory, and sit on material selection committees where the materials of their publisher, which conform to their theories, are being considered. But should such a committee be denied the professional judgment of such experts if it decides there is a conflict of interest? Often, also, ambitious young teachers who have their eye on becoming future authors or editors, can be inclined to favor a company likely to be responsive to their proposals. But, should curriculum committees have members who never have published and never will publish?

As a result of attempting to deal with such issues, which are really part of the internal dynamics of educational publishing, educators have created a situation, at all times aided and abetted by those they have ended up favoring, which has helped a small homogeneous set of large multinational companies to capture the bulk of the market and to reinforce the formidable barriers educators have placed in the way of any other publishers attempting to enter the market.

The Internal Dynamics of the Market Place: Learning Materials Selection/Adoption Procedures

In an attempt to procure the best possible materials, each province has its own formal learning materials selection and adoption procedures. The two most frequent procedures are termed "limited prescriptions or authorizations," and "open listings." Two less frequently used methods are known as "contract development" and "self-publishing."

The limited prescriptions or authorizations method operates as follows:

1. As a result of pressure within and/or outside the profession and, in some provinces, as part of a predetermined schedule, the province decides to review the curriculum of a certain subject at a certain level.

2. A review committee, chosen from "the profession" and most often by the provincial ministry, is struck and, in most instances, recommends a curriculum revision.

3. A revision committee is then struck (often completely overlapping in its membership with the review committee) and a new curriculum guideline is drawn up.

4. Near the completion of this revision, drafts of the new curriculum are sent out to publishers asking them to submit materials for consideration.

5. At this point, a selection committee is formed (often again with the same members as the previous two committees and, in some provinces, not distinguished by name) to review the materials submitted.

6. Selection is made and a recommendation is forwarded in confidence to the political level of the ministry, the deputy minister or an associate deputy minister.

7. The recommendation is reviewed at that level and presented to the minister.

8. The minister reviews the recommendation and makes a decision.

The chart on page 78, taken from a British Columbia government document entitled *Curriculum Planning, 1979*, illustrates how at least one province describes its process.

Ontario uses open listings to encourage a vibrant, provincially based, but decentralized purchasing procedures. Districts, schools, and teachers choose their purchases from the "open list," *Circular 14*, a provincial document listing all student materials approved as appropriate for use in Ontario.

Ontario uses openlistings to encourage a vibrant, provincially based, but nationally oriented, educational publishing industry. The statute which is the basis of *Circular 14* states that materials used in Ontario schools must be written, published, and manufactured in Canada. Recently, the Ministry also has interpreted the statute to require "appropriate levels" of Canadian content.[1]

Ontario uses open listings because it has the size to do so. Since the province represents one-third of the English-speaking elementary/high school market, approximately 120,000 students per grade, it can command a multiplicity of good materials. Ministry officials also argue that to severely restrict choice, by using limited prescriptions or authorizations, would jeopardize the continued existence of a considerable number of publishers and, as a result, would have deleterious effects upon the educational value of products produced for the market as a whole over the long-term.

In certain circumstances, however, neither of the two procedures outlined above will attract suitable materials. In such cases, and sometimes for other reasons, provinces turn either to contract development or self-publishing.

The more commonly used of these latter two methods is contract development, a technique with a venerable history dating back to the days of Ryerson. At some stage of the curriculum review or revision process, it becomes apparent that no materials suited to the specific needs of the curriculum and province are available, or likely to become available. The province

Figure 2/Development of Provincial Curriculum–Sequence of Tasks

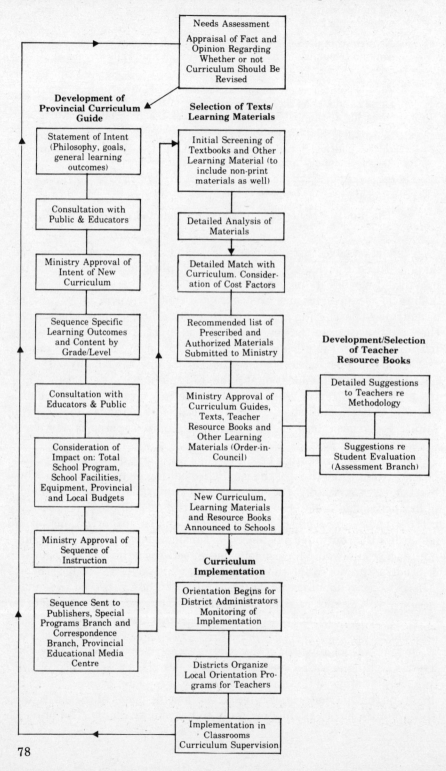

Needs Assessment

Appraisal of Fact and Opinion Regarding Whether or not Curriculum Should Be Revised

Development of Provincial Curriculum Guide

Statement of Intent (Philosophy, goals, general learning outcomes)

Consultation with Public & Educators

Ministry Approval of Intent of New Curriculum

Sequence Specific Learning Outcomes and Content by Grade/Level

Consultation with Educators & Public

Consideration of Impact on: Total School Program, School Facilities, Equipment, Provincial and Local Budgets

Ministry Approval of Sequence of Instruction

Sequence Sent to Publishers, Special Programs Branch and Correspondence Branch, Provincial Educational Media Centre

Selection of Texts/ Learning Materials

Initial Screening of Textbooks and Other Learning Material (to include non-print materials as well)

Detailed Analysis of Materials

Detailed Match with Curriculum. Consideration of Cost Factors

Recommended list of Prescribed and Authorized Materials Submitted to Ministry

Ministry Approval of Curriculum Guides, Texts, Teacher Resource Books and Other Learning Materials (Order-in-Council)

New Curriculum, Learning Materials and Resource Books Announced to Schools

Development/Selection of Teacher Resource Books

Detailed Suggestions to Teachers re Methodology

Suggestions re Student Evaluation (Assessment Branch)

Curriculum Implementation

Orientation Begins for District Administrators Monitoring of Implementation

Districts Organize Local Orientation Programs for Teachers

Implementation in Classrooms Curriculum Supervision

may then ask publishers for proposals containing an elaborate outline and an approximate price. On the basis of these submitted proposals, a publisher is awarded a contract to develop the materials. The successful publisher will most often be found working closely with a curriculum committee or a ministry consultant. The project may be financed in stages by advances from the ministry, or the publisher may borrow money based on the ministry contract. Once the materials are developed and classroom tested, they are automatically authorized for use. It should be noted that the minister makes the decision to go to contract development only after a review to justify this unusual step.

Some examples of recently contracted materials — a geology text on Saskatchewan; physical education kits in New Brunswick; grade 5 social studies; grades 7 to 9 Newfoundland literature; grades 7 to 9 literature anthologies; grade 10 Canadian issues; and grade 11 democracy texts, all in Newfoundland; and curriculum materials for grades k to 11 social studies in British Columbia — illustrate the kinds of projects where contract development has been used.

Ontario has extended the concept of development under contract with its Learning Materials Development Plan. Under that plan, Ontario identifies a considerable number of areas that have been ill-served by the "free market forces," under which traditional educational publishers claim to operate, and invites submissions from publishers, organizations, and individuals to develop materials to fill these gaps. The government offers applicants grants currently totalling approximately $400,000 per annum. After these materials have been developed, they are then reviewed for inclusion on *Circular 14*. They are not automatically listed.

The less commonly used method for alleviating the shortcomings of the normal development procedures is self-publishing. Here, the ministry, by itself or in conjunction with other government ministries, takes on the development and publishing of materials without the participation of an outside publisher. Publishers, of course, are unhappy to lose the business. The most dramatic example of self-publishing is the $8.38 million Heritage Learning Materials Project in Alberta. Smaller projects such as single texts are more common. For instance, the Council of Maritime Premiers has initiated a $1.5 million fund for 15 projects, mostly to be spent on other than print media. To cite one more example, the Northwest Territories has a materials production and development program with an annual budget of $300,000.

While self-publishing is quite uncommon in the print medium, and tends to run counter to what both publishers and educators see as the desired norm, the case is different for non-print materials. Every province has an audio-visual branch of the provincial education department to purchase and create materials for classroom use. In some provinces in recent years, these departments have undergone a metamorphosis and become visible producers and distributors of materials, both directly and indirectly oriented to the school curriculum. Four such producers are TVOntario,

Téléuniversité, ACCESS (the Alberta Educational Communications Corporation) and KNOW (B.C.'s Knowledge Network of the West).

While each of the above procedures for the development and adoption of learning materials may seem relatively rational and straightforward, there are a number of oddities about the process as a whole. Curriculum committees may take years to develop a new curriculum but ask for the submission of proposals for the design of materials in as little as three weeks and published materials within six months to one year! Moreover, curriculum development may consist largely of a review of what is already published rather than a consideration of basic educational goals and means. As a result, publishers often publish in anticipation of the decisions of curriculum committees. They lead as much as they follow, and have a considerable stake in materials adoption decisions. As a consequence, they have evolved a number of different strategies to market and develop materials successfully.

Development and Marketing Strategies of Educational Publishers

There are four main development and marketing strategies used by publishers, plus two lesser used strategies. They are as follows:

1. "Co-development." This is a major development effort which involves extensive co-operation between the publisher and all levels of the educational hierarchy within the province.
2. "Grassroots development." In this area a publisher works with a small group(s) of teachers within a province(s) on a more limited project.
3. "Importing." This strategy consists in importing a product from a foreign market and then adapting it to the Canadian or a provincial market.
4. "Importing high-profile American government-inspired programs," that is, importing and adapting a program based on a major government-sponsored effort.
5. "Transplanting," a lesser used technique, is parallel to importing, but involves marketing a product developed for one province in another province.
6. "Contract development," the other lesser used method, has been explained above.

These strategies and methods flow into one another and really represent a continuum. Even the two most different, co-development and importing, become difficult to distinguish on close examination. They warrant close examination not because they cease to be distinguishable but because, under close scrutiny, it becomes apparent why the market is monopolized by the large multinationals and also how educators reinforce that monopoly.

1. Co-Development

Co-development is the marketing/developmental strategy most frequently used by educational publishers outside Ontario. For the most part, it is an extensive co-operative process which involves a tacit approval from the provincial government for a publishing company to select and work with teachers in order to develop and test new materials suited to the provincial curriculum. Often, the province in which co-development is most extensive is the one in which the authors or editors work. Co-development often takes place simultaneously in several provinces so the materials will be appropriate to more than one provincial curriculum. In undertaking co-development, the publishing company has continual contact with all types of educators in the province, especially with subject-area consultants in the districts and the ministry. But the province does not make any formal agreement to purchase or even to give preferential treatment to the resulting materials.

Co-development amounts to much more than its formal description implies. The process has no identifiable beginning. A company, its products, and its reputation become known through visitations to teachers, district consultants, curriculum co-ordinators, provincial directors of curricula, and members of the curriculum branch of the various ministries. At conventions of teachers, supervisors, and others directly concerned with the curriculum, the latest wares of publishers are on display while acquaintances are renewed and cocktails or dinners are offered.

Once the formal groundwork is laid (it is continuously maintained) and any necessary formal arrangements are made with the province, the publisher moves into the development process itself. Development is a long, drawn out affair, often taking three years from start to finish. The publishing team must appear competent but also have enough openness so that the educators involved feel they have contributed to the development of the series or book. The primary goal is to obtain good information about the appropriateness of the materials. But just as important is a secondary spinoff of the process. Satisfactory publisher–educator relations encourage educators to identify with the company's products and transmit their positive attitudes to their colleagues.

If the publisher is successful, this process of co-development can lead to a *de facto* adoption or approval of the publisher's material. How? While no formal prior commitment is ever made, and it is difficult to find a materials selection committee composed entirely of teachers or others who have participated in the development of the materials, it would also be surprising if the committee members did not have personal contacts with others who did participate. The selection committee, of course, knows that it will get warm support from those involved and their immediate colleagues if it chooses the co-developed materials. The committee is also well aware of the general informal opinions of ministry officials. In sum, when the time to choose a series comes, these and other lesser factors work in favor of the relevant publishing company at both the time of materials selection and the very early stages of curriculum review and revision.

2. Grassroots Development

Grassroots development involves a small-scale project, such as a single text or a set of supplementary booklets. In this case they are developed in co-operation with a limited number of teachers and subject-area consultants. Higher level educational bureaucrats are most often not included and may not be aware of the project. Although it is used most frequently in Ontario, because that province is a centre of development and because decision-making is more decentralized there, the grassroots method is certainly not confined to that province.

This method involves a publisher obtaining the commitment of a number of teachers and supervisors to "pilot"* and/or "field test" materials and review them critically. Once the publisher reaches the stage where the material is considered suitable for classroom use, the publisher can then expand his or her contacts among teachers and supervisors for an expanded series of "field tests."

After this stage, the publisher must begin to think about marketing. In the Ontario market, the publisher may build up a body of teachers who like the materials before submitting them to the ministry for inclusion in *Circular 14*. Once submitted, a publisher can then use the collected favorable opinions to negotiate to get the materials accepted and to keep them close to their first published form. Once accepted for listing on *Circular 14*, an acceptance which commits the province to buy one copy for each school which might use them, the real selling begins. That selling involves district, school, and teacher visits as well as out-of-province, provincial-level efforts. In other provinces, the publisher theoretically must await the time when the province reviews new materials for selection or authorization. But such events do not prevent "pre-promotion" at lower levels in the educational hierarchy. Interestingly, one of the problems that arises in provinces other than Ontario is that publishers spend a certain amount of time promoting their materials to teachers despite the fact that a central body selects and adopts the materials. Provincial officials are sometimes at pains to point out where the authority for decision-making on learning materials lies. In a letter dated 20 June 1978, the deputy minister in Newfoundland wrote as follows:

---

*"Piloting" consists basically of classroom testing, but often under the watchful eye of educators and publishers not normally found in the classroom. Such presences can, of course, create positive results, not as a function of the materials but as a result of extra effort and attention. "Field testing" leaves the teacher more on his/her own, hoping that the quality and effectiveness of the materials themselves will be more observable.

Circular to Publishing Companies

I wish to bring to your attention the policy of our Department governing the authorization of text books. Under Section 59 of the Schools Act (attached) you will note that all texts require the approval of the Minister of Education before being introduced into our schools.

With the frequent visiting of Company Representatives to our local District Offices, the practice of offering free materials, including basic texts, on a class basis is becoming a concern to us at the Department. This practice encourages Districts, who are so disposed, to use texts which have not been officially approved.

Accordingly, we are requesting that Publishers discontinue such offers and that requests for basic texts be directed to the Curriculum Section of the Division of Instruction.

C. Roebothan
Deputy Minister[6]

A cultivated market for a rejected set of materials is not a happy situation.

3. Importing

Importing is a strategy used frequently by educational publishers outside of Ontario. It is not used often in Ontario because imports would normally not be listed in *Circular 14*. As with co-development, it is employed primarily, but not exclusively, by the traditional, large, and foreign-owned educational publishers. Small Canadian-owned companies, acting as importing agents, sometimes also adapt and market imported materials. Formally speaking, the publisher imports materials from another country, usually the United States, and attempts to sell them in one or more province of Canada. At one stage or another the materials also are "Canadianized." While the process has been discussed in Chapter 2, the following extract is a reminder of the very basics involved.

("Deke" for "Delaware")

Back in 1975, the Macmillan Publishing Co., of New York published the attractive *Macmillan Dictionary for Children.* . . . Collier Macmillan Canada Ltd. now has published *The Canadian Dictionary for Children* (768 pages, $13.95 cloth). . . . We know it is "uniquely Canadian" (as the Collier Macmillan publicity releases state) because it includes such entries as "muskeg", "Canada goose", and "Doukhobor". It is not American because it does not have entries for "White House", "Star-Spangled Banner", or "Memorial Day". But in fact, this new *Canadian Dictionary for Children*, is virtually the same book as its five-year-old American Counterpart. . . . To compare the two books page by page is fascinating (also easy, because almost all the items can be found in identical columns on identical pages). Obviously many of the American plates were used unaltered to print the Canadian version. It is intriguing to see how neatly some of the Canadian additions replace the American deletions, for example, the American dictionary has entries for all 50 states. In the Canadian version, "Alaska" is replaced by "Alberta", "California" by "Calgary Stampede", "Montana" by

"Montreal canoe", "Delaware" by "deke" (yes, "deke") and so on. This
is so cleverly done that hardly a column of print is thrown out of line.

Perhaps this enforced parallelism restricted to some extent the
Canadianizing of the dictionary's contents; there are some curious omissions. "Stanley Cup" is an entry, but not Grey Cup, "Red Rivert cart",
but not Conestoga wagon, "shorthorn" and "longhorn" but neither
Holstein nor Hereford, "larch" but not tamarack, "saskatoon" but not
elderberry, "soybean" but not rapeseed.[3]

The importation of already developed materials and ensuring their selection is nearly as involved as co-development. However, the effort centres
on marketing instead of development. The marketing job is a large one.
The first step is to contact provincial officials and make review copies
available. Most commonly, contact is also made with school district officials
at the same time, no matter what the provincial policy on selection. A rep*
might then make himself or herself available (or someone else with a
greater educational background) to schools for workshops to explain the
materials. Ginn used a dynamic, slick slide show and lecture in teacher
workshops emphasizing the art work of the readers to sell its *Reading 360*
and *720* in British Columbia.

Getting teachers or districts to "field test" the materials is also a major
accomplishment and effective selling device. The school boards and teachers
who field test imported materials are roughly equivalent to those who work
on a co-development. With a slightly different set of interests, they also
act as agents for the particular materials which they field test. Why?
Because in field testing teachers develop teaching aids and lesson plans
for the program, and acquire skills in using the materials. In sum, they
develop a vested interest in the province's decision, even if only based on
an attempt to be efficient in their investment of effort. This is perhaps why
Newfoundland found it necessary to be insistent in their instruction to
publishers. In a second memo to the presidents of publishing companies
dated 8 August 1979, the Deputy Minister of Education, C. Roebothan,
wrote:

> As indicated in a previous memo, the supplying of core texts at the
> district level is considered unethical by the Department. Identification,
> evaluation and recommendation of such materials is the prerogative
> of our curriculum committee, using criteria which have been approved
> by the Division of Instruction.[4]

4. Importing High-Profile American Government-Inspired Programs

Importing high-profile American government-inspired programs is as much
a passive contract method as an importing method. During the 1960s in

---

*The sales personnel of publishers who work "in the field" are referred to formal-
ly as publisher's representatives and informally as "reps." I shall, for the sake
of brevity and also to avoid ambiguity, refer to them as reps. This serves to
distinguish them from all others acting on the publisher's behalf.

the United States, teams of high-profile scholars (Nobel prize winners and the like) were well-funded by government to participate in curriculum development to improve the overall level of sophistication in a particular subject where authorities believed materials were inferior. After the government-funded scholars developed these programs, publishers bid for the right to publish, market, and distribute the material. In Canada, D. C. Heath (Canada), a subsidiary of D. C. Heath U.S.A. and the Raytheon conglomerate, gained distribution rights for what came to be known as PSSC Physics (Physical Science Study Committee), BSSC Biology (Biological Science Study Committee), and Chem Study (Chemistry Educational Materials Study).*

Programs such as these tend to sell themselves. In their development phases, they become well-known to the educational community as something rather special. They are discussed and reported upon at North American educational gatherings, are often centred around a prestigeous American university, and are as much a curriculum outline as a published program. Thus, for a curriculum committee to consider such a program seriously, it would begin that consideration with the initial curriculum review. By deciding that the curriculum outline of such a program was the one it wished to recommend, it would have tacitly decided to adopt the materials associated with it. Consequently, it might not seem particularly useful for the committee to then put out a call for other submissions of materials.

5. Transplanting

Transplanting, commonly called "adaptations" in the industry when adjustments to the materials are required, involves a publisher attempting to sell products in a provincial market other than the one for which it was developed. Most often, the publisher tries to sell to other provinces products developed for the Ontario market.

The major difference between transplanting and importing is that adaptation does not involve deletions or replacement of U.S. references with Canadian facts and figures, but rather tailoring the materials to the particular characteristics of a provincial curriculum. Also, in contrast to a recognition of the need to adapt imports, publishers tend to argue (by reason of economic necessity) that one Canadian edition is enough. But whatever occurs regarding adaptation, given the size of the Ontario market, "Canadian" materials are most often developed in Canada for the Ontario market and transplanted to markets other than Ontario. Provinces other

---

*Actually, for a time, Copp Clark acted as Heath's agent in Canada when these programs were first brought to Canada. However, in the common pattern of the type of company and the time, Heath decided to set up its own branch plant to distribute these materials. Having achieved a presence in the marketplace thereby, it then began to publish specifically for the Canadian market.

than Ontario are fond of pointing out that they must choose between Ontario and the U.S. And why, they add, should they always choose Ontario?

6. Contract Development

Contract development is really not a publisher's strategy, since it is fully controlled by provincial ministries. But many publishers and their organizations, especially the Association of Canadian Publishers (ACP), which represents the Canadian-owned publishers, have pressured provinces to use contract development as frequently as possible because it removes the financial barrier that prevents the small publisher from participating in the market. The Canadian publishers represented by the ACP claim that they are equally as capable of organizing authors, editors, consultants, and teachers willing to field test, etc., as are the multinationals. They also argue that, if provincial ministries planned curriculum innovation with sufficient lead times, they could easily work to reasonable deadlines to create and produce new materials. Provinces would then not have to buy "off the shelf" and, additionally, their products would reflect the cultural sensibilities which small and medium-sized Canadian-owned publishers have developed through their trade lines.

Contract development, as explained previously, amounts to financing by the province following the successful submission of a publisher's proposal. However, contract development is not without its politics and skulduggery either. Prior contracts with the ministry and the position of the senior editor of the contracted publisher may have been factors in the awarding of the contract for elementary social studies materials in British Columbia some years back, for example. In the case of a grade 6 P.E.I. and Atlantic history contract, only local publishers were invited to submit proposals. In New Brunswick a multinational was chosen to publish a provincial history on the basis of a proposal, but mostly because, following a lucrative adoption, it put forward an offer difficult to refuse. The official explanation is that the contract was granted on the basis of the proposal and the company's established reputation.

Monopoly in the Market Place: The Overall Market Structure

As educators have attempted, albeit with limited success, to create an internal market dynamics guaranteeing the selection of good materials (and free from unwarranted favoritism towards single companies), they have succeeded in erecting financial barriers which have, until very recently, prevented all but the very large companies from participating in the educational market. In other words, the nature of the educational market requires the participants to be highly capitalized to gain entry because only highly capitalized publishers can cope with the "safeguards" educators have introduced. But the restrictions are not completely educator induced.

The large, highly capitalized publishers have used their favorable position to persuade educators that only they, as a group, are capable of producing materials of "the highest quality."

What Have the Traditional, Large Educational Publishers Trained Educators fo Expect?

As pressure to revise a curriculum mounts, a publisher needs to be apprised of the situation so a decision to develop new materials can be made and personnel chosen, well before a curriculum committee defines the curriculum, let alone calls for submissions. The publishers must be able to identify various educators who appear capable, articulate, and are likely to affect the design of the new curriculum or are capable of designing a new program.

Co-development requires the services, not continuously, but at frequent, intermittent intervals over a three-year period, of people, usually reps, to undertake a series of tasks. Initially a set of contacts must by maintained with the ministry, authors, educational editors. Someone must also keep track of the feedback of teachers overseeing the "piloting" and undertake to provide introductory workshops. Several of these jobs may be taken on by one person with a variety of talents, but the requirements are certainly considerable and diverse. The publisher must underwrite all this and more; salaries, travel, complimentary copies, and so forth. There is also considerable risk. While a well-run co-development may all but ensure a major purchase, it can only *"all but"* ensure it. Educators become accustomed to this continual presence of the staff of various large publishers.

Educators have also come to expect to concentrate on "very big deals" as more and more publishers have moved to providing large "units" of materials. Not so very long ago, single texts were issued for single grades. These were then "packaged" with a teacher's manual or guide, one per grade. Subsequently, a "package," then called a series, consisted of a multi-grade set of texts with an elaborate teacher's or resource guide. These packages then became multi-component "programs" covering elementary years, while the guides began to evolve from resource guides to "management systems" designed for the materials. Most recently these programs have been expanded still further to encompass grades 1 through 8. Such a sequence of expanded packages is common across the curriculum, from language arts through science, mathematics, social studies, music, physical education, and so forth.

At what appears to have been a very useful meeting between publishers and educators in Edmonton in June 1980, Richard Lee, President of Ginn Canada, outlined the costs of preparing a K-6 reading series. First were development activities, including research (customer needs), scope and sequence development, and field testing. Second were production costs of the core components. Third were manufacturing costs. And fourth were post-publication costs, including pre-adoption activities such as customer calls, descriptive literature, workshops, samples, and pilot classes; and post-adoption activities such as workshops and customer service. According to his figures, the costs amount to a stunning total of over $3.5 million excluding interest on borrowed money.[5]

At a May 1984 meeting of the American Educational Research Association, it was reported that an integrated language arts series now costs $14 million to develop. While some of the difference between this sum and the Canadian figure is accounted for by inflation, it is also an indication of the value of "invisibles" passed from the parent to branch plant, thereby aiding the competitiveness of the branch plant. Invisibles include the managerial procedures to develop new series complete with piggy-backed supplements and so forth. The passing on of such invisibles is what makes co-development and importing points on the same continuum.

These very big deals involve what might be considered the core of the curriculum: language arts, mathematics, science, and sometimes social studies. As "packages" have increased in grade span, publishers have also ventured further into providing supplements to guide both teacher and student through the basic materials. Workbooks have been supplemented by pre-tests and post-tests designed to show the most miniscule advance or learning. Computers can analyse any aspect of the actual text a student studies. Textual characteristics can then be described as elements of the scope and sequence of the materials and designed into minutiae for pre- and post-tests.

As a result of such ventures into the educative function, educators now expect publishers to provide leadership in the definition of what should be taught and how. Teachers and education bureaucrats also expect high-ranking theoreticians to be part of the development team so publishers oblige, even if it means paying someone for the use of his or her name rather than for the work they put into developing the materials.

Still another implication of publisher leadership in the design and teaching of the curriculum is the tacit limitation placed on the breadth of concerns which become the legitimate horizons for an expert teacher in the field. For instance, one might think curriculum designers of literature programs would be quite concerned with the relationship between the course of study they prescribed and its relationship to world and Canadian literatures and cultures. However, a report on the state of the language arts curricula of the provinces, undertaken by the curriculum branch of the Province of Manitoba for the Council of Ministers of Education, takes quite a different perspective:

> Classroom materials (particularly literature) and the criteria of materials selection are under examination by a variety of groups and individuals across the country. This issue requires serious consideration. Criteria of selection must be rationalized to give maximum support to the achievement of the language arts goals.[6]

While the above might seem eminently justifiable, "language arts goals" are quite narrowly defined by curriculum committees in all provinces. For instance, Saskatchewan's senior English curriculum defines its goals in terms of four objectives: enjoyment ("reading is a course of lifelong pleasure . . . a well-told story delights the ear"), appreciation ("to appreciate a poem is to sense what an author is driving at"), philosophical concerns ("literature asks the kind of ultimate questions that every individual must ultimately ask"), and student writing ("wide reading among good writers is one of the best ways of enabling a student to develop a style of his own").[7] Such a perspective describes the reader–author interface as the meeting of two minds, two individuals unmediated by culture. It shows little concern for what the author has to offer the reader in placing him or her in his or her culture. Such a philosophy is typical. In British Columbia, for instance, a cultural concern is Goal 13 of the 14 goals of the province's English curriculum.[8]

The very big deals, which the large publishers have encouraged, are also made within a very short time period — the period between a call for materials or proposals for materials development and the selection of materials. Both as a result of a continuing presence in the field and as a result of being oriented to very large "units or packages" of materials, traditional educational publishers must develop materials well before curriculum committees call for submissions. Therefore, they must have the ability to submit major programs within a relatively short time, as little as three weeks for a proposal complete with sample chapter and layout, as little as six months for a major program. This ability to anticipate the market has become a criterion for legitimacy and therefore participation in the market. In a sense, it can also be thought of as a reward for providing educational leadership in curriculum development. More crudely, but at times not unrealistically, it can also be seen as a reward for having the guts, that is, the financial backing, to play in this high-stakes poker game.

Educators are also moving into yet another costly procedure with tacit approval of the large companies. From time to time major programs that have been adopted in one or other of the provinces have failed miserably in the sense that teachers simply do not use them. This situation has been defined as a "problem of implementation." To solve this "problem of implementation," the provinces are moving towards longer periods of inservice training of teachers before actual adoption, with mandatory participation of both the ministry and publisher in the implementation process. While the educational merits of such a procedure can be recognized, the financial implications mean publishers are going to have to carry their development debts for that much longer and, in the end, will charge that much more for their materials. Large companies and their subsidiaries are in a position to do so. For smaller companies, such a procedure represents just one more hurdle to stumble over in attempting to participate in the market.

When these short time lines and long development periods are combined with what is expected in a submission, market participation becomes very restrictive indeed. To elaborate a little, educators feel it legitimate to make choices late in the production sequence,* that is, when a book is essentially in its final form. By the time the materials reach this choice point the publisher has made a considerable investment not only of money but also in the content and approach of the materials. In effect, by demanding so much in order to make a choice between materials, educators are opting for an "off the shelf" item rather than one "made to measure" their particular curriculum. They seem unaware that by making such a late choice they severely constrain their ability to affect the form of the materials they purchase. The whole effort of curriculum development is meant to define the "measurements" they want their materials to be "made to". Yet they then choose an item "off the shelf". In addition, scratch a non-Ontarian with a comment in favor of interprovincial co-operation on the acquisition of materials and it is not long before comments like "Ontario will not dictate our curriculum," and "the provinces must exercise their educational responsibilities, that's democracy" come oozing out. The publishers have done an admirable job in persuading provincial educators that their B.N.A. Act-endowed freedom of choice can best be realized in the free, provincially divided market of an oligopoly of big business.

The predominance of very big deals means educators are opting for products which can only be provided by large companies who produce for the mass market. Educators believe such an option will maximize "quality". Most have yet to be convinced of the very real restrictions the mass market places on the approach to each subject in the curriculum. They also seem oblivious to their role as consumers, with a fragmented, that is, provincial, power base compared to the national and international power base of the producing multinational publishers. They also appear to expect, and even require, normal mass marketing cosmetics in order to be convinced of the value of their purchases. Four-color printing has become minimal for most publishers. Illustrations, to supplement text, which cost as much as or more to develop than the text, are also *de rigeur*. Pieces of "research," complete with tables and looking like an offprint from a scientific journal, along with facsimile four-color printings of the text, are common in promotional packages. Consultants and editors names are displayed as endorsements of the program. All sorts of supplements are "piggy-backed" on the basic text. Each is claimed to be integral to the success of the materials. Layout and titling such as "Starting Points" in Reading, Language, and Mathematics are all put to use in developing brand loyalty.

---

*In making such a statement, I am aware that educators may be fairly incapable of understanding what the nature of the final product may be, unless they actually can see it.

Where do all these induced expectations end? They end in one hyphenated word, "teacher-proof." Highly capitalized projects undertaken by large companies venturing further and further into the classroom are leading the big publishers to claim more and more responsibility for whether and how much the child learns. This is partially to the relief of some educators and much to the consternation of others. It enables self-justification, through the creation of testing programs, and promotes the self-fulfilling prophecy that publishers are more capable than teachers of "promoting learning." By providing successively more services, publishers will ultimately be successful in diminishing a teacher's ability to teach without such aids as elaborate pre-tests, post-tests, skill exercises, remedial aids, and so on, all purchasable components of what is referred to as a "management system." Publishers, in their testing programs, already banish failure merely by interposing the concept of "expected success rate."

As Bruno Bettleheim[9] has pointed out, today's readers introduce a very much smaller vocabulary than their forebears. U.S. readers of today introduce only 28 percent of the vocabulary introduced fifty years ago. Because the success of the publisher depends in his terms not on how successfully he educates children but whether his materials and services are bought by educators, he has a vested interest in developing materials which a maximum number of children can succeed in mastering, along with an extremely sophisticated measurement system for the plotting of minute progress, a kind of insurance policy. This maximizes the success rate in terms of test performance and goes some distance to ensure further product purchase. Such statements as Bettleheim's become merely interesting perspectives rather than being indicative of fundamental flaws in the whole process. Increased publisher control over the learning process also means that such companies can begin to use their full potential to develop products and advertising, which create needs for new products which, along with more advertising, create new needs for new products which, along with more advertising. . . . And so the autonomous commoditization process goes, in society and in education.

Who Are Canada's Educational Publishers?

Five very large firms dominate the English Canadian educational publishers market. Based on the 1969–1978 sales figures of six provincial book bureaus representing 30 percent of the market (British Columbia, Alberta, Saskatchewan, Manitoba, New Brunswick, and Nova Scotia, collected by Pepperwood Inc.),[10] those five are:

Publisher	Ownership	Percentage of Market Share
McGraw-Hill Ryerson	McGraw-Hill USA	12.5

Gage	Affiliated with Scott Foresman and now owners of Macmillan Canada.	11.4
Holt, Rinehart and Wilson	CBS USA	10.5
Addison-Wesley	Addison-Wesley USA	8.4
Ginn Canada	Xerox USA	7.9

Other major participants are:

Nelson Canada	International Thomson Organization	4.3
Macmillan Canada	Now owned by Gage	4.2
Prentice-Hall	Prentice-Hall USA	3.7
Copp Clark Pitman	Pitman UK	3.3

Together these nine firms account for 66.2 percent of the market. A further eleven firms, each of whom have between 1.0 and 2.5 percent market shares, account for an additional 18.4 percent of the market, bringing the overall total to 84.6 percent.

The activities represented by the Canadian elementary/high school or elhi market are fairly small potatoes to these giants. The size of the conglomerates, of which Holt, Ginn, and Nelson are a part, is vast. Most Canadians are well aware of the holdings of the International Thomson Organization in department stores (Simpsons and The Bay), newspapers (The Thomson Chain), and North Sea Oil, not to mention Nelson. "Smaller" firms such as McGraw-Hill, Prentice-Hall, and Addison-Wesley do $1 billion, $353 million, and $80 million respectively in business each year. Although two of the top nine firms, Nelson and Gage, are based in Canada, all nine are multinational companies. In fact, of the twenty top companies listed by Pepperwood Inc. in its report on publishing, only Clarke-Irwin, Book Society, and Fitzhenry and Whiteside could be said to be Canadian-owned, nationally oriented companies. The first two are now one company.

The Small Canadian Publishers

The traditional role of the publisher has been that of a mediator. He* brings to an audience the works of those he publishes. He provides a means for a culture to communicate with itself. However, the job contains a creative aspect. Every choice the publisher makes has a cultural consequence. Should he decide to bring no materials to public light dealing with certain subjects and should his fellow publishers decide to follow his example, the culture effectively supresses knowledge of that aspect of its identity. Every publisher has a cultural responsibility. Every publisher brings to his cultural role an understanding of the culture within which he operates.

---

*Meaning, most definitely, both he and she, throughout this paragraph.

During the 1970s, in fact with the publication of the Ontario Royal Commission on Book Publishing in 1972, what has been called a "new wave" of publishers was recognized. These small publishing companies were created by the talented young Canadian authors and editors of the late 1960s who found themselves with no vehicle to bring their opinions and writing on Canada, or from a Canadian perspective, to the public. They challenged and defeated the notion that Canadian trade publishing could be carried on only with subsidization based on profits from foreign imports. These publishers have been encouraged over the years, first by cultural funding from the federal government and more recently from the various provinces. They have also been recognized by cultural commentators and institutions. Their output, as of 1979, represented approximately 12.5 percent of the market but some 49 percent of domestic sales of Canadian-authored books. Some 68 Canadian firms, with a list of over 50 titles, existed in 1980 as opposed to 14 in 1970. Of those 68, 22 are based outside of Ontario as opposed to 3 in 1970, a growth of nearly 10 percent.[11]

While their cultural value has been recognized, their structural inability to make profits as an industry has also been noted. Little by little, schemes have been devised to ensure their continued existence. The basis upon which they initially received assistance is the same one which has justified its continuance and expansion through to the present day. As the Ontario Royal Commission put it, no sovereign country can afford to let foreign entities control such an important means of communication and creation of original ideas as book publishing. Furthermore, the realities of the Canadian market are such that reasonable profits cannot consistently be made through the publication of original contributions to literature, the arts, and scholarship. Therefore, since government controls that market place through import laws, the allowance of foreign investment, copyright law, and so on, it is incumbent upon government to shoulder the cultural responsibility of seeing to it that works of cultural value be published by and distributed amongst Canadians. The growth of the Canadian-owned sector over the past fifteen years, the public recognition it has received, and the sales it has generated are a tribute to the energy and abilities of the publishers, to the, at times, reluctant recognition of governments of the necessity to take action, at least to ensure the sector never dies, and to the interest Canadians have in their own culture.

Educators have not seen themselves as having similar responsibilities, at least not until very recently. As we have seen throughout this book, the standard view of educators is a narrow one. It is that the educator's responsibility is to choose, on behalf of students, those materials which most ably allow the student to acquire the skills and concepts of the discipline in question, a discipline defined within the milieu of U.S.-based "international" professions and organizations. Such a context is not likely to stress national or regional cultural perspectives.

As a result, educators as a whole are not inclined to view that something is fundamentally wrong if schools are full of textbooks which, by continual reference, laud the scientific achievements of the American empire. They see Americans at the forefront of "science" and us as their partners.

Under such a thought regime, small publishers have had little success in finding ways around the effective barriers to enter the educational marketplace.

However, these barriers, too, show signs of permeability. It appears educators are seeing the wisdom of a made-in-Canada education, if only for economic reasons. In certain limited circumstances contracts have been let to small Canadian publishers. These contracts have permitted the publishers to demonstrate what they can contribute. British Columbia, Alberta, Ontario, Quebec, Prince Edward Island, and Newfoundland all have limited schemes which encourage some participation of small Canadian trade publishers in their markets. As for the publishers, they are educating themselves through their associations about the educational market, while at the same time forming co-operative mechanisms which are mutually beneficial to their gaining entry to the market.

But dark clouds still loom on the horizon. The new communication technologies ushered in by the silicon chip, that is, microcomputers, videotex, videodiscs, satellite transmission, all have the potential of creating a market for educational materials which is even more exclusive and non-Canadian than educational publishing. The new communication technologies become economic only when the market served is vast. Electronic formats require even larger start up costs than does print. Distribution, on the other hand, and on a mass scale, is extremely cheap. If educators continue to be passive in accepting the organization of the market which is convenient to the dominant participants, and at the same time doggedly insist on the right to make separate and uncoordinated choices, that is, to preserve a fragmented market, the chances of a continued development of any kind of cultural or Canadian foundation to the curriculum will be minimal if not entirely absent.

Summary and Conclusions

In an attempt to procure the best possible learning materials for their classrooms, educators in all provinces have set up formal review and evaluation procedures for selecting new learning materials. Publishers have responded to these procedures by developing a number of different strategies designed to ensure that their materials receive the best consideration possible. One major element of all publishing strategies is anticipation of the demands of provinces so that publishers can respond quickly to calls for materials. Indeed at times, publishers' materials may be used to develop curriculum outlines rather than vice versa.

These strategies and selection procedures have together led to a situation which favors one type of publisher, the well capitalized, large company, often a foreign-owned branch plant. Two infrequently used "selection procedures," contract and self-publishing, place all publishers on an equal footing, the first by removing financial barriers, the second, by exclusion. But so dominated is the market by the branch plants that they have been successful in persuading educators that it is primarily they who are legitimate and capable educational publishers. Yet many of their products fall far short of being ideal, especially culturally ideal. Excluded from educational publishing are numerous Canadian-owned publishers of varying sizes, sensibilities, and locations. The latter are the very publishers who are broadly recognized as playing an essential cultural role in Canada and are almost totally responsible for the publication of serious original Canadian fiction and non-fiction.

Footnotes

1. J. Fraser, "The Circular 14 Story," *Orbit* 49, 10(4), 1979, 8-10.
2. C. Roebothan, "Circular to Publishing Companies," Department of Education, St. John's, Newfoundland, 20 June 1978.
3. M. A. Smith, "A U.S. Dictionary gains Landed-Immigrant Status by Substituting 'Deke' for 'Delaware'," *Books in Canada,* February 1980, p. 21.
4. C. Roebothan, "Memorandum to Presidents of Textbook Publishng Companies," Department of Education, St. John's, Newfoundland, 8 August 1979.
5. R. Lee, "Book Production: Ramifications and Problems," in G. H. Bevan, *1980 Publishers' Conference: Proceedings,* Calgary, 23-24 June 1980 (Edmonton: Curriculum Branch, Department of Education).
6. Language Arts/English Consultants, Manitoba Department of Education, *Canadian Language Arts/English Curricula* (Toronto: Council of Ministers of Education, September 1979).
7. Saskatchewan Department of Education, *Curriculum Guide*, Division Four, English 10, 20, 30, Regina, 1975.
8. B. C. Ministry of Education, *Secondary Guide,* p. 3, Victoria, n.d.
9. B. Bettleheim and K. Zelan, *The Child's Fascination with Meaning* (New York: Random House, 1982).
10. G. Scott, *English El-Hi Publishing in Canada, 1980-1986* (Toronto: Pepperwood, 1980).
11. R. MacSkimming, "Trade Publishing in English Canada," paper presented at *Book Publishing and Public Policy Conference,* Ottawa, April 1981 (Toronto: Association of Canadian Publishers).

5: Strategies for the Entrenchment of a Canadian Curriculum

Introduction

The purpose of this book to this point has been to portray the degree to which schooling in Canada is integrated into the culture of the country. Chapters 1 and 2 outlined the extent to which concrete Canadian cultural realities are introduced in language arts and English literature and social studies across Canada. Chapters 3 and 4 discussed the constraints placed upon the creation and transmission to students of that curriculum content. Each chapter has concentrated upon those elements which appeared most crucial to the central purpose of the book. In Chapter 1, elementary reading series and the choice of literature at the secondary level were described. It was concluded that publishers have been left in control of the content of elementary readers and, for the most part, have designed that content to suit their business interests rather than the cultural interests of the nation. At the secondary level, educators have asserted their authority and responsibilities in establishing the parameters on what is to be studied. Unfortunately, however, cultural matters have gone unattended.

Chapter 2 indicated that all provinces tend to agree that elementary social studies should introduce children to an expanding horizons approach from a personal, regional, and national base. However, two anomalies exist in the application of that philosophy. The first is the generic approach to expanding horizons. While on the surface the approach appears sound, an examination of the actual materials shows them to be bereft of cultural content. The second anomaly is to be found in provincial curricula. In various provinces an ordered sequence of courses is interrupted or left incomplete. Neither of these anomalies is justified in statements of intent by the provinces. More positively, any trends which can be seen in recent changes suggest that the provinces are on their way to developing

Canadian-based, logically sequenced, elementary social studies designed to expand upon the concrete, culturally based horizons of the pupils as they progress through the grades.

At the secondary level in social studies Canadian content is being inserted into curricula to an increasing extent in the form both of full courses and as points of reference for broader discussions, for example, the British Columbia curriculum revisions. While such a situation deserves praise, the learning materials being developed for these new curricula show a major shortcoming. Essentially, while Canadian content is included, the provinces put forward no underlying philosophy specifying a logical sequence of priorities in introducing Canadian content in secondary social studies.

The examination of the education profession and specifically teacher training in the third chapter concluded that cultural context is sorely neglected. Teacher training programs fail to deal explicitly with the cultural nature of education. An analysis undertaken of the backgrounds and professional activities of education professors suggests that such a failure is partially attributable to the training origins, and hence the academic concerns, of the profession as a whole. The increasing participation rates of faculty with Canadian citizenship and Canadian training was noted. However, no evidence exists of a relationship between increased Canadian hiring and the enhancement of a cultural presence in teacher training.

In the exploration of educational publishing and learning materials selection policies in Chapter 4, a detailed explanation was provided illustrating the interaction between educators and publishers in the development and selection of materials. The major implication of this interaction is that the market has been restricted to large international publishers who have adopted standard, mass marketing principles in the creation and sale of their products. In itself, this has led to the downplaying of distinctive cultural content. Excluded from educational publishing are the vast bulk of Canada's trade publishers who are responsible for almost all of Canada's original fiction and much of its non-fiction.

It is important to note what has not been, but which might have been, done in addressing the issues of the preceeding chapters. The research and commentary of this work has not sprung from a vacuum. In part, as noted in the introduction, it has been inspired by people who and projects which have addressed and continue to address the same central issue of this book. Across the country are teachers, education department officials, and education professors who have developed or promoted materials which pedagogically surpass materials normally used in schools. They surpass the materials we have discussed because they are built upon the concrete, personal experiences of the students who use them.

While passing reference has been made to a few such projects, lamentably the time and resources available to this study prevented any systematic reporting upon these valuable efforts. Indeed, perhaps one of the outcomes of the publication of this study will be a concerted attempt to make these projects known so that they may be used more widely and inspire further development of methods and materials.

The overall conclusion of this book is that, in spite of recent compensatory efforts, schooling remains quite out of touch with the everyday realities of Canadian culture. This is especially so in the way teachers are trained, in the manner in which educational materials are developed and selected for use, and in the teaching of language arts and English literature. The specific shortcomings which lead to this overall conclusion have been identified below.

Language Arts

At the elementary level in language arts, educators, acting through curriculum committees, have had little to say about content. As a result, large publishers and their editors-in-chief have had control over content and, for the most part, have let the mass market rule.

Control over content cannot be left in the hands of the publishers of elementary readers. The single, particularly compelling, reason for this is that these publishers are multinationals whose market interests are at odds with including and promoting distinct cultural content. In so far as these publishers exclude concrete culturally relevant information, their materials are culturally undermining and therefore pedagogically weak.

The emerging trend towards the inclusion of cultural and hence Canadian content and writing must be considered a bare beginning. We must insist upon content both of interest and value to the child and of value to the culture. Considerations of content must be the foundation for the teaching of language arts. This requires a fundamental reorientation on the parts of educators and publishers in choosing material. They must develop methods for identifying materials which are culturally enhancing and simultaneously engage the literary imagination of the Canadian child. The short-term solution is to appoint persons with cultural responsibilities to curriculum committees. The long-term solution requires that educators come to see the role of education in a cultural context.

Just as control over content cannot be left in the hands of multinational publishers, so access to the elementary reading market cannot be restricted to such companies. Small literary publishers and their authors and editors are the repositories of our literary heritage and our seers to the future. It does not make sense to inhibit the ability of these writers and publishers to participate in the elementary reading market. At the very least such inhibitions remove the threat of new, vibrant participants. As a result, it becomes very easy for those who now monopolize the market to publish what is purely convenient and profitable.

Initiatives of some provinces to include Canadian-written, -published, and -manufactured trade books as supplements, along with their increased use of contract publishing, address this problem to an extent. A more bold and the next necessary step is to allow these supplements to challenge fully the position of the "technologized" reading series by creating opportunities for teachers, together with authors and publishers, to use these supplements as foundations to reading programs.

Such a challenge would begin a much needed process of evaluation of the dominant philosophy of teaching reading intrinsic to all reading programs of all large educational publishers. Large publishers and professional educational experts have been taking reading step by step towards a technologically precise, skills-oriented exercise. The publishers control content, amount learned, and evaluation procedures. With such an overreaching control, they have come to address pedagogical value within the framework of their business interests. For example, small advances of the student are precisely measured to prove the value of the materials. To allow these supplements to challenge presently used reading series would begin to answer the question of how much of this fancy technology is merely restrictive both of content and market competition.

Literature

The major problem in the study of English literature is to determine what Canadian work should be introduced, at what level, and in what quantity.

It is heartening to see the goodwill which is developing in the country towards Canadian writing. However, if Canadian literature is to become a vibrant part of English literature curricula, to say nothing of its becoming the cornerstone of those curricula, students must enjoy what they are reading, teachers must know how to enhance the enjoyment of Canadian writing, and authors need to be aware of students as an audience. Students cannot be persuaded to read works of cultural significance when those works lack the elements which make literature engaging and compelling to them. At the same time, teachers are not best prepared for teaching and enjoying Canadian literature on a background of studies which excludes Canadian writing. And authors cannot write for students if they pay no attention to the lives and minds of Canadian adolescents.

Students and authors could be brought together through programs of writing and comment upon each other's work. Such programs both within and outside the curriculum might prove quite popular. Room might also be made for teachers in such programs. However, teachers are more likely to benefit from Canadian writing being included as a requirement in their training.

In essence, the study of literature, as it is presently practised, places a forbidding distance between Canadians and literature. Methods must be found to help students realize how a piece of literature grows out of culture, how it is crafted into a work of art, and how, in turn, such works enhance what is distinctive and what is best about a community. At the grassroots level, bringing teachers, authors, and students together in programs designed to foster knowledge of, and respect for, authorship addresses the issue. At the level of the nation a much different technique is required.

If one new Canadian major literary work were to be taught in grade 11 in each province; if that work were to change each year; if the work taught had been published in the previous three years; and if that work were chosen for each province by well-respected bodies in a well-publicised manner, then Canadian writing, Canadian education, Canadian literary reviewing, and the diversity which is Canadian culture would receive a tremendous animation.

Elementary Social Studies

There is every sign that all provinces are moving towards the adoption of the type of regionally based, nationally sensitive curricula in elementary social studies discussed in Chapter 2. They would be well advised to develop explicit policy statements encompassing this tendency both for their own and for the benefit of the public. For three stumbling blocks in achieving such curricula exist. They are curriculum design, learning materials, and teacher attitudes.

The development of satisfactory curricula and, following that, good learning materials will take some time. If the publishers of such materials are Canadian-owned and lack extensive industry experience, their shortcomings will provide considerable temptation for educators to fall back on imported known entities in both curricula and materials. At least three generations of curricula and materials will probably be required before excellent results evolve. This process of development can be aided greatly if provinces recognize their shared goals explicitly and attempt to rationalize their distinctive goals not only in terms of their own philosophy but in terms of the philosophies of other provinces. Also, they should make a concerted effort to learn about and take guidance from the development of materials and curricula in each other's jurisdictions.

However, in planning and developing curricula, it should be recalled that elementary teachers must keep up to date not just on one subject but on several. If teachers are to change emphases and develop new teaching techniques, then they must believe that a shift towards regional and national content is both valuable and long term. If teachers are expected to display extra effort during implementation, then they must detect a genuine overall shift in educational philosophy before they will wholeheartedly commit themselves to adjusting both their content and their techniques.

Secondary Social Studies

Change in senior social studies should focus on the curriculum primarily, and secondarily on the materials which emerge in response to that curriculum. Each of the provinces has embraced a minimum of one course on Canadian history or Canadian studies at both the junior and the senior high levels. However, a philosophy basic to determining appropriate content does not appear to have emerged. It is true, at the junior high level, that history is made more personal and therefore more social; and at the senior level, both curricula and texts lean towards a formal constitutional history. However, such differences in emphasis have emerged because of the beliefs of educators about the cognitive or thinking capacities of the students rather than from cultural considerations. The question apparently unaddressed is "What should Canadians with a high school education know about their country?" Perhaps it is for this reason that Ontario's orientation to Canada and Canadians in grades 7 to 10 has already been criticized by the Secondary Education Review Project.[1] As with the elementary level, the senior grades will require several generations of materials and curricula to achieve a suitable level of excellence. Again, an easy retrenchment must be guarded against.

The benefits the provinces can gain by learning from the efforts of each other and coordinating curricula is doubly important in secondary social studies. Interprovincially coordinated curriculum development allows a greater investment of time and resources both on the curriculum and on materials, resulting in higher quality in both. Coordination does not mean identical curricula across the country nor the use of identical materials. But lack of coordination can create situations in which educators set aside their own pedagogical priorities in the name of budget constraints. For example, the apparent frustration of Nova Scotia or Manitoba at having to use imported materials for their grade 9 British history and their grade 7 world geography respectively, rings hollow when one realizes that they have two additional choices. The first is to consider the pedagogical necessity of offering a course for which no other province sees the need. The second is to fund the development of suitable Canadian materials under contract.

Training for Educators

Substantial benefit would be gained if every teacher had a background in the cultural, political, social, legal, and historical dimensions of Canadian education. Considerable advantage would also accrue if all teachers had a background in the study of Canada or things Canadian within their disciplines. Without such a dual background teachers lack valuable cultural foundations crucial to the teaching of their subject to Canadian children in Canadian schools.

Besides resolution to act, two factors stand in the way of bringing about such a reorientation in training. The first is the concerns of student teachers and the pressures of teacher training. The second is the training and attitudes of education professors.

In an education program spanning a number of years there is ample time to introduce the dual background in Canadian realities described above. However, it may be that teachers would be a considerably more interested audience, especially for a more intensive exploration of the general contextual background of Canadian education, after they had spent several years in the classroom. On the other hand, in a one-year program, beyond some arts or science university training or a bachelor's degree, it is quite difficult to make room for contextual courses and gain the interest of student-teachers given the immediate necessity of job-related skills. Perhaps a re-evaluation of one-year training programs is desirable. Included within such a re-evaluation could be a consideration of in-service training and education on a mandatory basis.

As for education professors, the expertise needed to provide teachers with the Canadian disciplinary and contextual background referred to does not now exist in sufficient quantity in faculties of education. Nevertheless, its development could be undertaken fairly speedily by retraining. However, the real power in such a retraining of professors would only be gained if it were accompanied by a thorough Canadianization of teacher training in education faculties and of education as an academic discipline. That can be accomplished by a variety of means. Rewards such as research grants and chances to consult with colleagues over Canadian questions are quite enticing.

Building the Canadian identity of the profession would also undoubtedly help in this area. Encouraging the hiring and, given tight money, the exchange of faculty with a variety of provincial backgrounds would promote a pan-Canadian dimension to faculties as working units. With a continuing preference for hiring Canadians (provided any hirings take place), these initiatives would stimulate some reorientation. If all of these were combined with a broadening of the control of teacher training programs to reflect the public interest, the possibility of a speedy reorientation of teacher training to local conditions and pan-Canadian realities would be increased.

It should be pointed out that we are *not* proposing that education professors cease drawing upon and initiating international contacts and developing their work according to the rigors of international scholarship. What is proposed is that a conscious policy of teacher training be developed which takes into account the cultural nature of education. The difference in interest between scholarship *per se* and primary and secondary education as instruments of socialization must be recognized.

The Publication and Selection of Learning Materials

Four types of initiatives have been taken in this country to deal directly and indirectly with the domination of large international publishers in the market and a correlative lack of Canadian content. They are: first, the

Learning Materials Development Fund of Ontario; second, provincial self-publishing (where Alberta's Heritage Learning Resources Fund is the most dramatic); third, contract publishing; and fourth, information dissemination. These four types of initiatives favor Canadian publishers and Canadian material. However, they have their limitations and can be improved.

The Learning Materials Development Plan

In areas of marginal profitability, the Ontario Ministry of Education, through the Learning Materials Development Plan, has decided to encourage the development of Canadian materials (to fill out the mandate of the statute basic to *Circular 14*) rather than to opt for imported materials, highly imperfect materials, or no materials at all. Already accustomed to small projects and profit margins, small and medium-sized Canadian publishers were quick to step in. In essence, the financial barrier to market participation had been removed for materials designated as priorities by the administrators of the fund. To provide a sense of the identities of the users of the fund, in 1980 some thirty-three projects were aproved. In addition to individuals and public bodies, these projects were the efforts of eleven different Canadian-owned publishing companies and two branch plants. On the basis of the experience of previous years, a good percentage of these projects promise to be a success.

The Learning Materials Development Plan represents a major, stimulative intervention in the educational market. It provides an entry vehicle for small Canadian publishers which does not exist in the open market. In terms of the participation of Canadian-owned companies, it has been such a success that the Association of Canadian Publishers (the association of the Canadian-owned publishers) has been lobbying with other provinces to develop parallel plans. Knowing this, it is important to bear in mind that the plan is open to all publishers. Grants are approved on educational criteria without favoring Canadian publishers.

Self-Publishing

Self-Publishing by provincial ministries of education has been waning in popularity for some time. Although they have never cast it aside, and indeed, as mentioned in Chapter 4, some provinces have expanded their efforts tremendously in non-print materials, both educators and publishers see a legitimacy in private publishers wanting to choose whether to take on all projects a ministry has to offer.

The atmosphere was changed considerably with Alberta's announcement of the $8.38 million Heritage Learning Resources Project. It should be emphasized here that all the project materials which were developed, published, and distributed in 1981-82 free to Alberta classrooms were Canadian-content materials. The importance of the project is twofold. First, it was a direct intervention in the provision of Canadian content materials. Second, the project was also a stimulus for all levels of education in the province from the professors, through the authors, editors, and consulting publishers, to the teachers and students. The project was an act of province-building centred on educational materials but oriented to cultural, employment, and talent development as well. Already it has contributed significantly to the tone of both social studies and literature as it is studied in Alberta.

Self-publishing remains an option for other provinces,[2] although they tend to use it only when there is little hope of publishers developing materials. As a result, most often only materials for geographically unique minorities tend to be self-published. Two examples are reading series for Indians and Inuit developed by the Northwest Territories,[3] and a film on the Micmac developed by Nova Scotia.[4] At times such projects can lead to further development of materials under contract as it has done with Prince Edward Island's collection of essays, *Readings in Prince Edward Island History*, edited by Harry Baglole.[5] An elementary Island geography and history is now being developed by a small Canadian-owned publisher largely on the basis of Baglole's earlier success.

Current projects aside, it is important that the provinces hold on to the ability and the opportunity to publish materials on their own. There is always a certain difference between the possibilities of the market place and educational necessities.

Contract Publishing

Contract publishing has already been introduced, discussed, and current examples given. Contract publishing is important and extremely useful for two reasons. First, it allows educators to specify exactly the materials they wish rather than having to deal with the vagaries of the market place. Second, in a single dramatic move, it breaks down the financial barriers which prevent small Canadian-owned companies from entering the market.

No consumer group is well served by a monopoly held by a group of companies which have a similar corporate structure. By moving to include the whole of the heterogeneous Canadian publishing industry, room is created for genuine educational advances rather than spurious marketing innovations. With contract publishing, educators have the responsibility fully on their shoulders for developing Canadian materials.

Towards Contract Publishing

One other move can be taken by the provinces towards favoring a broader range of publishers than currently participate in the market. Two provinces which have used this method are Quebec and British Columbia. It amounts to providing extensive information to all potentially interested publishers about needed materials. Quebec has created sets of documents they call a *"Devis"* or *Direction du Matériel Didactique.* These publications give a detailed outline of the requirements for suitable materials and invite publishers to develop and submit such materials.

An Overview

The single most effective policy for the generation of culturally valuable materials would be an explicit statement on the matter. For example, the following statement could be adopted by each province:

> "Learning materials will emphasize Canadian realities in a manner appropriate to the position of education as a major official institution responsible for passing on Canadian heritage to Canadian children and adolescents."

With such a policy in place, along with the stimulative and market access-broadening policies now being used to a limited extent by several provinces, for example, contract publishing, an abrupt change in the nature of learning materials would occur. That change would be very much to our cultural benefit.

Between Publishers and Educators

The above policies deal with the structure of the market. Its internal dynamics also require attention. The generation of good learning materials takes place in an environment of dynamic and continuous interaction between educators and publishers. To attempt to limit that interaction in the name of fairness amongst individual publishers is a mistake. Opportunities for publishers to interact with educators must be broadened to include all publishers who might gain from the experience. Also, in times when both corporations and governments spend great sums of money marketing and advertising themselves, it is difficult to limit publisher–teacher interaction to materials development rather than promotion. Nevertheless attempts must be made in order not to penalize those companies who cannot compete on an equal footing in promotion.

The Federal Contribution to a Canadian Cultural Education

The federal government has been a traditional participant in Canadian education through transfer payments. In addition, at least through such Commissions as the Massey Commission and the Bilingual and Bicultural Commission, it has shown a policy concern. Following 1975, it embraced the report of the external examiners of the Organization of Economic Cooperation and Development. Its favorite paragraph has been the one quoted in the introduction:

"In distinction from most other comparable industrialized countries, Canada has neither produced a politically motivated educational reform, rooted in a conception of the country's future nor has Canada blocked such reform. . . .*Canada has exceptionally active programs . . . that are . . . derived from no explicitly stated, overall national conception of the country's interests.*" (my emphasis)[6]

Using this report as justification, along with statements of its general responsibilities in education, the federal government has developed policies in two areas which bear on Canadian content. Firstly, it has supported Canadian studies in itself. Secondly, it has supported national associations of educators concerned with Canadian Studies at all levels of education. In July 1981, it announced a three-year, $3.8 million National Program of Support for Canadian Studies. In April 1984, it renewed this program with an $11.7 million grant designed to expand upon what had been established by the 1981 program. Thirdly, it has, through its agencies (for instance, the Science Council of Canada), set up specific programs "to assess the scientific and technological resources, requirements and potentialities of Canada."[7] It has also, through another of its agencies, the Social Sciences and Humanities Research Council, set up a system of grants it has labelled "strategic" and declared Canadian Studies to be a "strategic area."

The second area of support in which the federal government has been active is in publishing. While federal support for publishing has been in existence for more than a decade, and a variety of programs has evolved, that support has been directed to the trade sector. In announcing a $4.5 million support program to sixty publishing firms for the period 1979-80, the then Secretary of State, Francis Fox, confirmed that commitment:

"The book publishing sector represents a vital cultural industry for Canada. Our aim is to work towards the objective of substantially increasing the industrial capability of the Canadian book publishing sector at home and abroad. I am confident that this cultural/industrial approach offers a good medium-term strategy for realizing the full potential of this essential cultural industry."[8]

However, one major innovation in that program was its specific concern with educational publishing. The explicit statement of the minister was:

". . . the purpose of this assistance (for learning materials) is to slow and, if possible, halt the displacement of Canadian textbooks and related learning materials in Canadian schools by foreign publications. In the first year of the program's operation, $1,500,000 has been made available for this purpose."[9]

In light of the total expenditure on education in Canada by all governments ($20 billion per annum [10]), these programs are small indeed and have the deficiency of failing to improve the relative position of smaller Canadian publishers. But they are, in combination with other federal support programs for publishers, at least a recognition of a problem which is growing rather than diminishing.

Corporations on the School Doorstep

Of the myriad of influences on education which the future holds, two especially powerful ones bear some discussion in the context of this study. The first is the role of corporations in the schools. The second is the influence new technologies will have on the form and content of education.

With publishing companies increasingly becoming subsidiaries of larger conglomerates who have non-educational interests in retaining access to the classroom, and with general cutbacks in educational funding, it will be very tempting for educators to sell audiences of school children to corporations for the price of providing educationally valuable materials along with product propaganda. The corporations are already on the schools' doorsteps if not in the classrooms.

One particularly noticeable example involves McDonald's of hamburger fame. McDonald's has developed a series of school workbooks dealing with nutrition, ecology, and economics.[11] Besides introducing McDonald's to school children and maintaining their presence in the children's minds, the workbooks demonstrate that the hamburger giant is concerned with: (a) the health of children who crave, via images, their products; (b) the neatness of communities in which they operate and where their excessive wrappings form a significant pollution; and (c) the ability of children to make sound economic decisions in an increasingly money-dominated world and where McDonald's represents the interests of the mass market. Not content with the relatively softsell of the workbooks, the company has followed the lead of numerous other corporations and produced a self-promotional film called *Mecology,* that is, "me" plus "ecology." While they market this film on their own and below the price one would pay for the film stock, other companies tend to pay distributors on the basis of the number of times they lend out a film at no charge to the viewer. Of course all this activity and hidden pay-offs and charges fudges the lines between legitimate classroom access and access for commercial purposes. It is a line which must remain clear.

Towards a New Technological Future

The attempts of large corporations to gain access to the classroom leads directly into the second issue which will have a major influence on education in the future: the use of new technologies such as microcomputers, videodiscs, and so on. Current technological developments are making information creation and dissemination a frighteningly large part of economic and cultural activity. With these developments Canada is extremely vulnerable to becoming the victim either of the hodge-podge of vested interests who will be buying and selling access to various audiences, or of the tendencies and conveniences of the technology itself, a technology which has at its base one imperative — economies of scale.

Educators who are enthusiastic about bringing electronic communication technologies on stream tend to fall into two camps. The first group comprises those who love the machines and the possibilities they offer for inventing, testing, figuring out, exploring the limits of the machines, and teaching others to do the same. The second group is made up of those who see the advance of civilization through a melding of technology with human creativity. Both points of view ignore the cultural perspective. If their enthusiasms win the day, all the battles which have been fought over Canadian content will have to be refought in the new technologies. Only, with the increased initial investment new technologies require for the development of software, the stakes are far higher for the software publishers and the hardware manufacturers.

With that much more to lose, they will be that much more vigilant in guarding their own interests. And with that much more initial investment required, Canadian producers will be at an even greater disadvantage than they have been in the print medium. If a very slick microcomputer program or videodisc is available for the study of *Catcher in the Rye* in contrast to a locally produced simple program or videotape for *Who Has Seen the Wind?*, which will be studied?

A Closing Proposal

If, in spite of recent efforts, schooling at present remains out of touch with the everyday realities of Canadian culture, is the above analysis and are the recommendations which arise from it sufficient to address such a general problem? It appears that were the present analysis accepted in its entirety and were all educators to change their philosophy to one consistent with that which underlies this book, a general cultural reorientation could be achieved.

However the likelihood of such a conversion of the education profession is small. Consequently, it is tempting to call for the establishment of a commission on "Children and Canadian Culture." Such a commission could assemble an exhaustive description of the content and the sources of ideas to which Canadian children are exposed in and outside of education. It could then call for an assessment of the situation and proposals for modification. Handled well such a commission could be both grand and exciting. And one of its major spinoffs would be to animate discussion by Canadians of our socialization process much as the Berger Inquiry animated the people of the Mackenzie Valley.

However, establishing an effective commission is fraught with difficulty. At what level would it exist? the federal government? the provinces acting in concert? the federal government along with the provinces? Are any of these likely possibilities? Would Quebec participate? The problems, even with the establishment of the commission, are enormous. And would any significant action be taken? Or could educators be lulled into thinking that government was taking care of the problem?

What might be more feasible would be a major research project designed with much the same goals in mind as were mentioned with respect to the commission. Its purpose would be to describe the socialization of Canadian children in all its facets. Once such a report were published, the widest possible grouping of educational and non-educational associations could convene a major symposium to discuss the findings of the report and inaugurate a policy-planning committee whose responsibility it would be to call for recommendations and to produce a policy report for future action.

Besides developing policy, the second major purpose of such a procedure would be to develop a cultural consciousness in both educators and Canadians. It is a lack of cultural consciousness which has allowed education to develop into the system which has been outlined here. Only when all bodies with responsibility and/or concern for education, from the federal government through the provincial governments, school boards, school trustee associations, teachers, and other educators and their associations, parents and their associations, publishers and their associations, to political parties themselves, come to think of education in a cultural framework, only then will Canadians gain the strongest possible pedagogy and the firmest foundation for survival and development.

Recommendations

Just as opting for a commission into "Children and Canadian Culture" is tempting, so is it also tempting to propose an extensive set of recommendations each of which addresses one aspect of the many problems which have been identified in this study. A more pragmatic approach would be to make major crucial recommendations on the assumption that the fewer recommendations there are, the more serious attention they will receive. Also, by making general recommendations, one can hope for a certain diversity in their development and application.

General Recommendation

1. Whereas this study has argued that the formal elements of schooling in Canada in two crucial subject areas are quite out of touch with the everyday realities and sensibilities of Canadian culture, *it is recommended that a general, widely based, and intensive effort be mounted to orient curricula, learning materials, and teacher training to these Canadian cultural realities and sensibilities.* While some specific recommendations follow dealing with the various areas which have been the focus of this study, in keeping with a "strategic grants" philosophy, a major piece of research should be funded

to identify the content and the sources of ideas to which growing Canadian children are exposed in and outside their education. The initiation of this research should also involve appropriate professional associations who would undertake to promote awareness and discussion of the compiled description and, following that, the development of a policy document designed to ensure that Canadian children, in the course of growing up, are introduced to the realities and sensibilities that are their heritage.

General Educational Recommendation

2. Given the inevitable delays in setting up such a research project and following it with the development of such a broad policy document, *it is recommended that educators act expeditiously through their professional associations, provincial departments, and teacher-training institutions to develop clear and concise policies which affirm the cultural nature of education.* Recognizing that education is a dynamic entity, ever changing with the development of new curricula, new learning materials, new members of the profession, and newly evolving ideas, plans can be laid both for immediate change and for confirming long-term change.

Specific Recommendations

Elementary Language Arts
3. *Educators should re-establish control over the content of elementary reading material for a number of cultural purposes.* A priority is to ensure that they contain appropriate Canadian content in sufficient quantity. Criteria must be established to ensure that both the culture and children are well served by the content of the curriculum and learning materials. While the level of Canadian content need not be quantitatively rigid, educators should be convinced that a Canadian sensibility is being introduced as a point of depature for other information and perspectives.

A second purpose is to maintain a priority for concrete, useful content suited to the aim of informing Canadian children of the immediate and broader communities of which they are a part. A third purpose is to break down barriers to the introduction of Canadian writing into elementary language arts materials. A fourth is to ensure a clear separation between the interests of the dominant publishers and educational interests.

The primary vehicle for the re-establishment of this control is provincial curriculum committees. However, at present, such committees lack cultural sensitivity. Therefore, educators must look for models of committees which have cultural sensitivity such as those of the Canada Council or some provincial cultural-funding bodies. The principle of recognition of legitimate interests either by committee membership or procedure must be adopted.

Secondary Literature

4. *The principle of introducing Canadian writing and Canadian sensibilities to Canadian students in the context of related literatures and sensibilities and through various genres should be enshrined in the study of literature in secondary schools. Special emphasis on the cultural nature of the study of literature should be added through the choosing and teaching of a new Canadian major literary work in grade 11 in every province.* To ensure the greatest success in such an enterprise, efforts need to be undertaken to identify both the central concerns of contemporary adolescents and the social ideas from which maturing young people would benefit. Individual literary works which explore these adolescent concerns and ideas, particularly appealing genres such as science fiction and biography, and especially successful teaching techniques must be identified. In addition, means must be developed to sensitize English teachers to their role as cultural mediators through both their training programs and professional specialty organizations. Underlying the above must be an enhancement of the cultural diversity of our country.

Elementary Social Studies

5. *In keeping with current trends in the area, educators in all positions should contribute to the development of fully rationalized regionally based, nationally sensitive elementary social studies curricula.* Intrinsic to this process is the avoidance of generic materials in favor of those which draw attention to specific, distinctive features of social phenomena. Educators should be aware that success may not follow first attempts and that considerable benefit can be gained by interprovincial cooperative efforts. In addition, teacher acceptance of this evolving focus may be slow in coming and require not only in-service training but also evidence of a long-term commitment to the perspective by educational administrators.

Secondary Social Studies

6. *Rationales basic to the teaching of secondary social studies which place Canadian information at the centre of their perspectives must be developed in all provinces to provide guidance for course offerings, the status of courses (mandatory or optional), and course content.* Once these rationales have been articulated, provinces should explore the benefits of cooperation in the development of curricula and learning materials. Provinces should be prepared to fund the development of new learning materials they deem necessary. Teachers, through their professional specialty associations, should be included in this process of redefinition and development at every level.

Teacher Training

7. *All teacher-training programs in Canada should be designed so that every graduate has both a thorough background in the cultural, political, social, legal, and historical dimensions of Canadian education and a background*

in the study of Canada from the point of view of at least one discipline. In order to achieve this goal, control over the design of teacher-training programs should be broadened to include community representatives. Professors should be encouraged through funding to orient their professional activities towards Canadian questions and should be offered retraining in areas of inquiry which deal with Canada. Continuing education programs for teachers could prove a useful vehicle to promote knowledge of Canadian realities as could generous funding for national associations and national symposia. Policies favoring the hiring of Canadians should continue and be supplemented by programs which introduce Canadian society and Canadian education to new young, faculty who lack such a background.

Learning Materials

8. *Educators should take the necessary steps to ensure that presently used learning materials are replaced by materials which are written, edited, published, and manufactured by Canadians and "emphasize Canadian realities in a manner appropriate to the position of education as the major official institution responsible for passing on Canadian heritage to Canadian children and adolescents."* Such steps might include the development or continuation of learning material development plans; contract publishing; provincial self-publishing; circulation of information specifying the requirements of learning materials; and non-print media producing, purchasing, and distributing agencies and interprovincial exchange programs. The restriction of promotional activities by large companies or subsidizing promotional activities of smaller companies and providing equal opportunities for local or Canadian publishers at minimum should also be included.

Federal Involvement

9. *The federal government should continue to support Canadian Studies through its various departments and agencies while encouraging the provinces to assume responsibility for at least some of these activities. Also, the federal government should continue to develop programs of support for a heterogeneous, regionally based, culturally strong, Canadian publishing industry.*

Footnotes

1. Ontario, Ministry of Education, *Secondary Education Review Project Report* (Toronto: Ministry of Education, 1981).
2. Saskatchewan Education, *Report of the Social Studies Task Force* (Regina: Department of Education, 1981).
3. J. A. MacDiarmid, *Dogrib Legends* (Toronto: McGraw-Hill Ryerson, 1972); also *Tendi Series* (Toronto: McGraw-Hill Ryerson, 1972). Originally published by the Department of Education of the Northwest Territories.

4. Nova Scotia Department of Education, *Mi'kmaq* (Film) (Halifax: Education Media Services, 1981).

5. H. Baglole, ed., *Readings in Prince Edward Island History* (Charlottetown: Department of Education, 1977).

6. Organization for Economic Co-operation and Development, *External Examiners Report on Educational Policy in Canada* (Toronto: Canadian Association for Adult Education, 1975).

7. Science Council of Canada, *Bulletin of the Science Education Study* (Ottawa: June 1980, p. 2).

8. Office of the Secretary of State, Press release, November 22, 1978.

9. Ibid.

10. Canada, Statistics Canada, *Canada Handbook* (Ottawa: Statistics Canada, p. 92).

11. McDonald's Corporation, *Nutrition, Action Pack* (Toronto: McDonald's Restaurants, 1978); *Ecology, Action Pack* (Toronto: McDonald's Restaurants, 1977); *Economic Action Pack* (Toronto: McDonald's Restaurants, 1976).